The Microsoft® Guide to

Managing Memory

with

DOS 5

The Microsoft® Guide to

Managing Memory

with

DOS 5

DAN GOOKIN

PUBLISHED BY
Microsoft Press
A Division of Microsoft Corporation
One Microsoft Way
Redmond, Washington 98052-6399

Library of Congress Cataloging-in-Publication Data

Gookin, Dan
      The Microsoft guide to managing memory with DOS 5 : installing,
   configuring, and optimizing memory on your PC / Dan Gookin.
          p.   cm.
      Includes index.
      ISBN 1-55615-381-3
          1. Memory management (Computer science)   2. MS-DOS.   I. Title.
   QA76.9.M45G66   1991
   004.5'3--dc20   91-23054
                                                                         CIP

Printed and bound in the United States of America.

   2 3 4 5 6 7 8 9   RRD   6 5 4 3 2 1

Distributed to the book trade in Canada by Macmillan of Canada, a division of
Canada Publishing Corporation.

Distributed to the book trade outside the United States and Canada by Penguin Books
Ltd.

Penguin Books Ltd., Harmondsworth, Middlesex, England
Penguin Books Australia Ltd., Ringwood, Victoria, Australia
Penguin Books N.Z. Ltd., 182-190 Wairau Road, Auckland 10, New Zealand

British Cataloging-in-Publication Data available.

Acquisitions Editor: Michael Halvorson
Project Editor: Megan E. Sheppard
Technical Editor: Jim Fuchs

Contents

Acknowledgments

It was way cool to be working with Microsoft on this project. Special thanks go to Mike Halvorson, who seems like a normal guy (even though he works for Microsoft); JoAnne Woodcock, the Goddess of DOS; Jim Brown, who bought me a beer once; Marjorie Schlaikjer, to whom I have yet to propose; Megan Sheppard, "Queen of the Quickie"; Jim Fuchs, tech weenie extraordinaire; and proofreaders Deborah Long and Shawn Peck, typographer Carolyn Magruder, and designer Kim Eggleston, who threatened grievous harm to this book if their names weren't mentioned in the acknowledgments. And thanks to artist Lisa Sandburg, who could never paint something as lovely as she herself is.

Outside the land of the world-famous carnivorous leopard slug, I'd like to thank Bill Brown of Qualitas; Charles McHenry of Quarterdeck; Kenny Jacobsen of Novell, Chicago; Matt Wagner of Waterside Productions (for reading and then sending back my Star Trek script); Debbie and Jerry just because; and the two publishers whose books suffered while I finished this magnificent tome.

(FREEDOM! FREEDOM! Can't you just smell all that extra RAM?)

Introduction

Memory management is a subject that has been avoided for way too long. Now the memory issue has exploded, and everyone is scrambling for cover. A few years ago there was only *expanded memory*. Then came *extended memory*. It was an $800 answer in Double Jeopardy: Which is which? Yet nagging questions still loomed: *What can I do with that memory? What makes it useful?*

And now, with the introduction of DOS 5, people who have long been avoiding the subject are staring it in the face. *How can I use all that extra memory in my computer? And what can DOS 5 do with that memory?*

Although DOS 5 doesn't perform memory management automatically, it does assume you know what you want; DOS 5 gives you options and lets you make choices based on your personal needs. Accordingly, no one-paragraph memory solution will work for everyone. But new commands exist that can be exploited. Consider the new DOS 5 command:

```
dos=high
```

That one line in your CONFIG.SYS file can help move some 50 KB of your operating system out of main memory.

DOS 5 has other tricks:

- The HIMEM.SYS device driver allows DOS 5 to access an extra 64-KB region of memory and opens the door to megabytes of extra memory.

- The Devicehigh and Loadhigh commands move device drivers and memory-resident programs out of main memory, giving you more memory for your spreadsheet, network, or Windows applications.

■ Third-party memory managers can be used with DOS 5 to make even more room available. The following is the output of the DOS 5 Mem command on a computer that is using a third-party memory manager:

```
753664 bytes total conventional memory
753664 bytes available to MS-DOS
736800 largest executable program size
```

Is This Book for You?

This book was written to help you get the most from DOS 5 and your computer's memory. It answers the following questions:

■ Exactly how is memory used in your computer?

■ How can you add memory to your computer?

■ How can you take advantage of all that memory?

■ What can DOS 5 do to optimize memory usage?

■ What are UMBs, and how do they increase available memory?

■ What are the XMS and EMS standards?

■ Where exactly is the HMA?

■ How does Windows fit into the picture?

■ What can be done with all that memory?

In addition, this book describes memory hardware—getting the most from your computer by using a RAM disk or a disk cache. To further illustrate how everything fits together, the final chapter contains several scenarios for adding and using memory on a variety of computers.

How to Use This Book

This book requires no science degree. The only requirement is that you be somewhat familiar with DOS. And you should wipe that stern look off your face. This book will clear up those dark, doubtful memory clouds over your head; you'll learn to get your full dollar's worth out of all that memory in your computer.

■ Chapter 1 provides an introduction to memory and microprocessors.

■ Chapter 2 describes how computers use memory. It also defines various terms for the different areas of memory in a computer.

■ Chapter 3 introduces the Mem command, DOS 5's way of telling you how much memory is available in your computer.

■ Chapter 4 is about adding memory to your computer—the physical installation of memory chips or memory expansion cards.

■ Chapter 5 concentrates on DOS 5 memory commands and how to use them.

■ Chapter 6 divulges the secret for moving device drivers and memory-resident programs out of main memory.

■ Chapter 7 tells you how a RAM disk and a disk cache can be used to speed up your computer.

■ Chapter 8 describes how to get the most from Windows under DOS 5.

■ Chapter 9 discusses DOS 5 and third-party memory managers.

■ Chapter 10 contains several "setup scenarios"—different computers in different situations and how to optimize each computer's memory under DOS 5.

■ The end of the book contains a glossary and a command summary—handy at-a-glance references that help demystify the subject of memory management.

If this book contains a secret, it is simply this: Memory management is not a skill that's limited to the computer elite or the programming priesthood. It's time for *you* to pull up a chair to your computer, crack your knuckles, and start putting all that memory in your computer to work.

Chapter 1

What Is Memory?

Memory is the place where the microprocessor, the computer's brain, temporarily stores data while you work with it. Memory lets you store your ideas, express your creativity, and do your work. The more memory your computer has, the more it can do.

This chapter describes the memory inside your computer. It's introductory material, starting off with a tour of your PC's inner workings, followed by a discussion of bits, bytes and kilobytes, and a description of how memory is controlled by the various Intel and compatible microprocessors. This chapter establishes the background for how memory works in the PC.

LOOKING UNDER THE HOOD

With a sweeping motion of your arm, clean all the clutter off your computer desk. You're about to take a trip inside your computer, peeking and poking and prodding, finding out where the memory, the expansion slots, and the microprocessor are.

Note: I know not everyone can suddenly pull the plug on their computer and visit Orville in maintenance to borrow a screwdriver. But if you can, go ahead and open it up! In the office, gather everyone around. Be bold.

Opening the Case

Before you open your computer, turn it off. Unplug it as well. (I speak from experience here. While I was working on a printer one day, a coworker happened to see it was unplugged. He dutifully plugged it back in while my fingers were inside. Trust me. Turn the computer off *and* unplug it.) You should also remove everything from the top of the computer's main box (*system unit*).

Now, move to the back and unscrew the screws that attach the cover to the system unit. (You might need to pull the system unit out, away from the wall.) You will find from two to six screws, generally at the corners of the system unit, at the top center, and maybe another on the bottom. They'll all be the same type of screw, usually a Phillips head. (Don't unscrew any screws of a different size.)

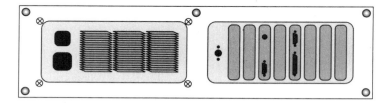

O   Remove these screws
⊗   Do not remove these screws

After you've removed the screws, pull off the cover: Slide it toward the front of the system unit, and then lift it up at an angle. (If the cover doesn't budge, you might have forgotten a screw, or the key on the front panel might be locked.) While pulling off the cover, watch out for any ribbon cables or wires that might snag. Pull slowly enough so that you can catch these and move them out of the way.

After the cover is off, set it aside.

Looking Around

Each PC is different inside, but all share similar parts. The inside of a PC contains one circuit board of electronics, usually made of green fiberglass and crawling with electronic "insects." Locate it at the bottom of the system unit. This is the *motherboard*. (See Figure 1-1.)

Look for banks of memory chips on the motherboard. They could be in a set of rows and columns of little black RAM chips called *dual in-line packages* (DIPs), or they might be standing single file on tiny cards called *single in-line memory modules* (SIMMs).

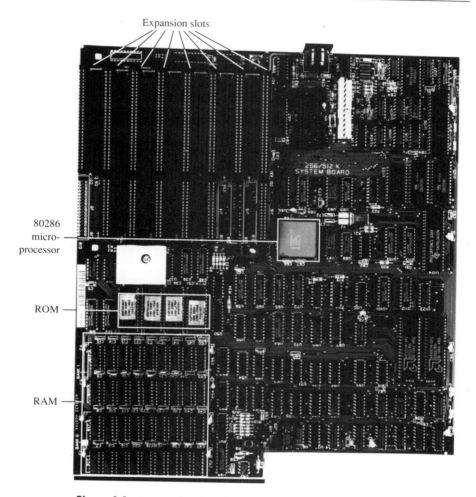

Figure 1-1. *A typical PC motherboard.*

Some motherboards, generally those in 80386 or i486-based computers, have special memory expansion slots. These are different than the standard expansion slots (near the back of the computer). Locate one now if you can.

Other items worth finding inside your PC are the power supply, which contains the fan and supplies power to the rest of the computer; the disk drives, both hard and floppy; expansion slots and cards; and the computer's battery and speaker.

Look for the microprocessor. It's a flat black chip—like a Keebler Fudge Stick with small metallic legs—either rectangular or square. On top of the chip you'll see numbers such as 8088, 8086, 80286, 80386, i486, V20, V30, and so on. Gently push any wires or cables out of the way if it's crowded in there.

Note: Not every system has a visible microprocessor. For example, the microprocessor in my Dell 386 is located under the hard disk and out of sight.

Finally look toward the back of the motherboard at the rows of expansion slots. These slots are connected to the computer's *bus*, a communications link between the microprocessor and other devices. Specially designed cards plug into these slots. One type of card you can plug into a slot is a memory expansion card. After the motherboard is fully populated with memory chips, a memory expansion card allows you to add more memory to the computer.

Close 'Er Up

That wraps up the tour of your PC. To put the cover back on, position it over the front of the system unit and carefully slide it back. Keep cables out of the way so that they won't snag.

Note: If you were adding memory at this point, you wouldn't put the cover back on. Instead, it's a good idea to test the memory with the cover off. That way you can fix any problems without repeatedly removing and replacing the cover. Be sure the power is off while doing this— never insert or remove a card or a memory chip while the power is on.

Push the cover back as far as possible. If it doesn't go all the way back, it might be improperly aligned; be sure that the lip at the base of the computer is inside the cover. Also, check the key to be sure it isn't locked, and check inside to be sure the cover hasn't caught any cables. Then insert and start tightening the cover screws. When you're done, simply plug the system unit in, connect the monitor, and turn the computer on.

BITS, BYTES, KILOBYTES, AND MEGABYTES

Memory is where your computer stores information. But how? How can something as lovely as a poem or as creative as an Escher illustration be stored electronically?

Computers know nothing of words, sounds, shades of gray, or perspective. What they do know is ''on'' and ''off''—the presence or absence of electricity. *On* is equal to about 5 volts of current; *off* is equal to no current. To us, the computer represents on and off in its memory with the values 1 and 0.

You can't get too far with only a 1 and a 0. These are the digits in the *binary* (base-two) system. Humans, probably because we have 10 fingers, use the *decimal* (base-ten) system, which uses digits from 0 through 9. A 0 or a 1 is known as a *binary digit,* which contracts to form the word *bit.*

A bit can store only one of two values: 0 or 1. Combining multiple bits increases the amount of information that can be stored. For example, 2 bits can store four binary numbers: 00, 01, 10, and 11. These are the decimal numbers 0, 1, 2, and 3. If you've never seen binary numbers before, this sequence may look a little strange. Why is 1 stored as 01, but 2 stored as 10?

Consider the decimal number 307. Each digit in the number is multiplied by a different power of 10: the 7 is the units digit (10 to the power of 0, which is 1—any number raised to the power of 0 is 1); the 0 is the tens digit (10 to the power of 1); and the 3 is the hundreds digit (10 to the power of 2). So the decimal number 307 is 3×100 + 0×10 + 7×1.

The binary system works the same way—only each digit is multiplied by a power of *2.* Consider the binary number 101. The digit furthest to the right is multiplied by 2 to the power of 0 (1), the next digit is multiplied by 2 to the power of 1 (2), the next digit is multiplied by 2 to the power of 2 (4), and so on. Therefore, the binary number 101 is 1×4 + 0×2 + 1×1, which is equal to the decimal number 5.

A *byte* is a group of 8 bits. It is the smallest collection of bits that the microprocessor can work with. This grouping allows 256 different combinations. (In general, the number of combinations possible by combining bits is 2 raised to the power of the number of bits in the group; 2 raised to the eighth power is 256.) Therefore, a byte can store a number in the range 0 through 255. The microprocessor knows the location, or *address*, of each byte in memory, and it can store or read the byte at any given address.

When you think of a byte in memory, picture it as storing one character of information. The word ''door'' requires 4 bytes of memory. A paragraph might require some 400 bytes; a page of text, almost 2000 bytes. The numbers grow and grow.

As you deal with more and more memory, other terms come into play. A *kilobyte* (KB) is 1000 bytes of information. (Technically, a kilobyte is 1024 bytes, but in the binary number system, 1024 is the closest power of 2 to the decimal number 1000.) A page of text takes about 2 KB of memory.

To store text, you need only a few kilobytes of memory. For example, no chapter in this book takes up more than 50 KB of memory space. But when you deal with graphics and sound, much more memory is required.

The number of bytes needed to store a graphics image is staggering. In the early days of the personal computer, no one dreamed of storing multicolored images in a PC—there wasn't enough memory! But with newer PCs that have millions of bytes of memory, today it's possible.

A *megabyte* (MB) is one million bytes of memory. Technically, it's 1024 KB (1024 times 1024 bytes, or 1,048,576 bytes, which is 8,388,608 bits—a mind-boggling amount). But this is nothing! An 80386 microprocessor can access 4096 MB of memory, or 4 *gigabytes* (GB) worth.

Memory storage is closely related to a computer's potential. The more memory your computer has, the more you can do with your computer. More memory opens up avenues for storing more diverse information, such as spreadsheets, music, graphics, and so on. The terms bits, bytes, kilobytes, and megabytes describe the quantity of memory your computer has.

MICROPROCESSORS AND MEMORY

Memory is necessary because the microprocessor, your computer's brain, really has no place to put things. Having enough memory has always been important. You would think the more the better. But the design of the microprocessor actually limits the amount of memory it can use.

One measure of a microprocessor's power is the width of its *data bus*. This is like an electronic data highway—the wider the data bus (the more ''lanes''), the more data can be moved at the same time. A microprocessor has both an internal and an external data bus. The internal data bus moves data between the internal components of the microprocessor. The external data bus is for communication between the microprocessor and other parts of the computer, such as disk drives, expansion cards, and memory.

Another measure of a microprocessor's power is the width of its *address bus*. The width of a microprocessor's address bus determines the amount of memory it can access. For example, the 8086, with its 20-bit address bus, can access 1 MB of memory. The 80286, which has a 24-bit address bus, can access 16 MB of memory.

The term *bits* is commonly used to describe a microprocessor's data bus width. For example, the 8086 is called a 16-bit microprocessor because it has an internal 16-bit data bus. The microprocessor in the first PC was an Intel 8088. The 8088 is a hybrid—it's known as an 8/16-bit microprocessor. This is because the 8088 has an external 8-bit data bus but an internal 16-bit data bus.

True, this is funky. The 8088's sister, the 8086, has an internal and external 16-bit data bus. But the chips required to support the 8086 cost more, so IBM went with the 8088.

Regardless of the technical differences, the 8088 and the 8086 both have a 20-bit address bus and can access 1 MB of memory. The maximum amount of memory the microprocessor can access is referred to as its *address space*.

All PC "clones" based on the original PC followed the same system design, which was limited by the 8088/8086's 1 MB of address space. Other design factors came into play, which is one reason why memory is so complicated in today's PC. (This is explained in the following chapter, "How Your Computer Uses Memory.")

Microprocessor	Bits	Megabytes	System(s)
8088	8/16	1	IBM PC, PC/XT
8086	16	1	Compaq
80286	16	16	IBM PC/AT
80386SX	16/32	16	PS/2
80386	32/32	4096	PS/2
i486	32/32	4096	PS/2
i486SX	32/32	4096	PS/2

The PC/AT came with an 80286 microprocessor, which is actually the grandchild of the 8086. (The 80186—Intel's next "generation" of microprocessor—was used in some computers, notably the Tandy 2000, but really offered no outstanding memory features over the 8086.) The 80286 has an internal and external 16-bit data bus. It also has a 24-bit address bus, which allows it to access 16 MB of memory.

The 80386 microprocessor—the PC's dream chip—has an internal and external 32-bit data bus. It's compatible with the 80286 and the 8086, but it has a 32-bit address bus, so it can address an astonishing 4096 MB of memory.

The best thing about the 80386 is its ability to exploit memory between 640 KB and 1 MB—an ability that DOS 5 uses to full advantage. Because of its power, the 80386 is quickly becoming the standard microprocessor for PC computing.

The 80386 has a little sister, the 80386SX, which has an internal 32-bit data bus and all the memory magic of the 80386. However, the

80386SX is rated as a 16/32-bit microprocessor; it has only a 16-bit data bus. The 80386SX is cheaper than the 80386 (also called the 80386DX), which makes a PC with an 80386SX an excellent alternative to a PC with an 80286.

The latest microprocessor to reign inside a PC is the i486. Although this has 32-bit data and address buses, it offers some extra power and features. For the purposes of memory, the i486 works in the same way as the 80386 and 80386SX. In this book, the term '386 refers to any PC with an 80386, 80386SX, i486, or i486SX microprocessor.

The purpose of this history lesson is to make you familiar with how a microprocessor's power is related to the amount of memory it can use. The problem is that DOS was written for the 8088 with its paltry 1-MB address space. Earlier versions of DOS treat a '386 like a fast 8088. That's not very efficient, nor does it take advantage of the full memory potential of the '386. This is why DOS 5 is different: It lets you have the memory and use it too.

HOW MEMORY WORKS

If you've always wondered how a row of flat chips and electricity can store information, the following explanation will be of interest.

There are two basic types of computer memory: *RAM* and *ROM*.

The bulk of your computer's memory is *random access memory* (RAM). RAM is memory that the computer can read from and write to. RAM is *volatile* memory—whenever you shut the computer off, any information stored in RAM is lost. There are two types of RAM: *dynamic* RAMs (DRAMs) and *static* RAMs (SRAMs).

DRAMs have a large storage capacity and a low power consumption. Their memory cells are basically charge-store capacitors that you can think of as incredibly tiny batteries. The presence or absence of a charge in a capacitor is interpreted as a logical 1 or 0. Because the capacitors tend to lose their charge, DRAMs require a periodic charge-refresh cycle—an electronic shot in the arm—to maintain data storage. This refresh cycle slows down the operation of DRAMs.

SRAMs store 1 and 0 using a different method—a method that doesn't require refreshing. They are faster than DRAMs but have a smaller storage capacity and are expensive to manufacture. For these reasons, SRAMs are rarely used in PCs. Most if not all the RAM chips in your computer are DRAMs.

ROM stands for *read-only memory*—memory that cannot be written to or updated. ROMs are not volatile: A ROM chip retains its contents even when the power is off. Because of this, ROMs are used to store special instructions (how to load the operating system at boot time, how to control a hardware device) or other vital programming code for your computer. Unless you get into some very serious programming, these ROM instructions are completely transparent to you: The computer finds and uses them when it needs to with no intervention from you at all.

A RAM chip is rated by how many bits it can contain. There are 16-Kb (kilobit), 64-Kb, 128-Kb, 256-Kb, and 1-Mb (megabit) RAM chips. But note that these chips store individual bits, not entire bytes. Why? Because RAM chips in IBM PC and compatible computers are arranged in *banks* (rows).

Because a byte has 8 bits, a bank should have eight RAM chips. On a PC, however, a bank has nine chips. Each chip supplies 1 of the 8 bits in the byte, and the ninth chip supplies a *parity bit*. The parity bit provides error checking on the other 8 bits, ensuring their reliability.

Note: Think of a 256-Kb RAM chip as a stack of 256,000-odd bits. In order to make 256 KB, you need eight (plus one) stacks of 256,000 bits. That's how one bank of 256-Kb RAM chips equals 256 KB of memory. The same holds true for 1-Mb chips; you need nine of them to make 1 MB of memory.

Four more terms will help you understand memory: *access time, wait state, interleaving,* and *cache memory.*

Access Time

Memory is rated for speed as well as capacity. The microprocessor is constantly writing and reading numbers to and from memory. For example, the microprocessor might want a certain number stored in memory location 100000. It takes a certain amount of time for memory to store the number and go through a refresh cycle. This delay is known as the memory's *access time*. Access time is measured in nanoseconds (ns), or billionths of a second. The lower the access time, the faster the memory.

Wait State

Ideally, the memory is fast enough to store the number and go through a refresh cycle before the microprocessor is ready to store another number. If not, the microprocessor must wait one or more clock cycles (sort of like electronic "heartbeats") for the memory to finish refreshing. Each clock cycle the microprocessor must wait is known as a *wait state*. Zero wait states, the optimal arrangement, means that the microprocessor doesn't ever have to wait for a memory refresh.

Interleaving

Memory chips are traditionally arranged in a row-and-column matrix, much like a spreadsheet. A particular memory address is located using a row number and a column number. With this arrangement, DRAMs just can't keep up with today's 33-MHz (or faster) microprocessors because of the time required for the refresh cycle. SRAMs are fast enough, but they are very expensive. Fortunately, a memory arrangement was discovered that minimizes the slow memory/fast microprocessor problem. This memory arrangement is known as *interleaved* memory.

Typically, a program accesses memory sequentially. If a program wants to store a number in memory location 100000, it will probably want to store a number at memory location 100001, then 100002, and so on. Interleaved memory therefore divides memory into two regions. The first region contains even-numbered memory addresses; the second contains odd-numbered addresses. These regions undergo memory refresh on different clock cycles.

Now when the microprocessor stores a number in location 100000, location 100001 is being refreshed. When the microprocessor stores a number at location 100001, location 100002 is being refreshed. This simple arrangement lets slower memory keep up with speedy microprocessors.

Cache Memory

Cache memory is a small amount (typically 32 or 64 KB) of very fast SRAM memory that sits between the microprocessor and the main memory. When the microprocessor reads data from or stores data in main memory, the data is stored in the cache memory as well. If the microprocessor needs that data again, it reads it from the cache memory rather than the slower main memory. Intel incorporates 8 KB of cache memory directly into the i486 microprocessor.

Because the cache memory contains SRAMs, it's expensive—typically adding $300 to the price of the computer. But the speed increase is dramatic. Buy a computer with cache memory if you can afford the added cost. Unlike the other kinds of memory we'll be discussing in this book, you can't add cache memory to your computer—you must purchase a system that already has cache memory installed because cache memory is an integral part of the motherboard.

Note: Be sure to check your computer's user manual before buying extra memory chips. It should list the size and speed of the chips your computer needs. It doesn't hurt to buy faster chips, but slower chips will cause unnecessary wait states and hurt all-around system performance.

None of these terms, nor any of the information in this section, is crucial to understanding how DOS 5 works with memory. If you want more information and happen to be in the Boston area, the Boston Computer Museum has an excellent display on how memory works. Visit the exhibit and see all of the museum if you're ever in Beantown.

SUMMARY

Memory is the temporary storage area for your computer. The amount of memory your computer can access is directly related to its microprocessor. The more powerful the microprocessor—the wider its address bus—the more memory it can access. The drawback used to be DOS, which forced device drivers, memory-resident programs, and applications programs to compete for memory space in the lower 640 KB of the 1 MB of memory accessed by the original PC's microprocessor. With DOS 5, that has changed.

- A bit is a binary digit and has one of two values: 0 or 1.

- Bits are grouped 8 to a byte.

- A byte can store one of 256 values. Conceptually, think of a byte as a character.

- A kilobyte equals 1000 bytes (technically, 1024 bytes).

- A megabyte (1024 KB) equals 1,000,000 bytes (technically, 1,048,576 bytes).

- The 8088/8086 microprocessors have an 8-bit or a 16-bit data bus, respectively. They can directly address 1 MB of RAM.

- The 80286 microprocessor has a 16-bit data bus and can directly address 16 MB of RAM.

- The 80386 microprocessor has a 32-bit data bus and can directly address 4096 MB of RAM.

Chapter 2

How Your Computer Uses Memory

It's idealistic to think of a computer containing 1 MB of RAM. There's something pure and surreal about 1 MB of clean, uninterrupted memory—like that endless, grassy fairway without a tree or a sand trap. Regardless, memory inside a computer simply isn't that smooth, contiguous bank of nine RAM chips. Instead, memory is separated and classified according to the computer's needs.

This chapter is about the arrangement of memory inside the typical PC. It's also about terminology, and when it comes to understanding memory, terminology is key.

THE PC'S MEMORY

When IBM designed its first microcomputer, the PC, it used the 8088 microprocessor. The 8088 (and 8086) can address 1 MB of RAM, meaning it has an address space of 1 MB.

IBM's engineers had to assign part of that address space to the necessary ROM and the rest to RAM. They decided that the lower 640 KB would be used for RAM and that the upper 384 KB would be reserved for ROM. When the PC made its debut, it did not have a full megabyte of memory, but the line had been drawn: Below 640 KB was for RAM and for use by DOS and applications; above 640 KB was reserved for use by ROM, the video adapters, and so on.

This is where the two basic terms for describing the PC's memory come into play: *conventional memory* and *reserved memory*.

15

- Conventional memory is the PC's basic RAM, from 0 KB through 640 KB. It is also referred to as *low-DOS memory*.

- Reserved memory is the memory area above 640 KB, reserved for ROM. It is also referred to as the *upper memory area* or *high-DOS memory*.

Conventional Memory

Conventional memory is where DOS loads and runs your programs. Lower conventional memory is reserved for use by the computer, but from about the 2-KB mark on up to 640 KB, you can run applications. This doesn't mean that you have the full 640 KB (or 638 KB) available for all your RAM-greedy applications, either. After all, DOS dwells in conventional memory, eating up anywhere from 18 KB to 90 KB depending on the DOS version.

RAM Cram

The proliferation of memory-resident programs peaked in the mid-1980s. At that time, just about every program could make itself resident, giving you instant access to the program at the touch of a hot key. Although few programs needed to be resident, making them so was a good sales gimmick.

The problems with memory-resident programs were many. First, no one standardized a way to create them. Programs would conflict, each trying to wrest control of the computer. Second, DOS didn't help, providing no rules or regulations for the horde of memory-resident (TSR) software. Finally, the memory-resident programs were using large areas of conventional memory—a condition known as *RAM cram*.

Eventually, the madness ceased. Today you can still find memory-resident programs, but most are utilities. The urge to produce the ''pop-up application'' has vanished. And with the advent of environments such as Windows and DESQview, there is less need than ever for memory-resident applications.

Atop DOS are some *data storage areas*—places DOS uses to manage any open files, plus any device drivers loaded with CONFIG.SYS and any memory-resident programs that AUTOEXEC.BAT loads. Ultimately, on top of it all, is your application and any files you've loaded for use with the application, such as a document or a spreadsheet.

In the worst-case scenario, with enough device drivers and memory-resident programs loaded, you might have only a few dozen kilobytes of conventional memory left over for running your applications. But is this enough?

The Upper Memory Area

IBM reserved the upper 384 KB of the PC's memory for future expansion or for ROM. The original PC used only a sliver of that memory for its BIOS, the Basic Input/Output System that provided the PC with low-level instructions for controlling peripheral devices such as disk drives and the keyboard. Another small portion was used for video memory, where the information to be displayed on the monochrome or color display was stored. And yet plenty of room existed for expansion.

Today, the upper memory area still hasn't filled with ROM. The first 128 KB are used for video memory: the monochrome, CGA, EGA, or VGA graphics systems in most PCs. The next 128 KB are reserved for installable ROMs such as video ROM and the hard-disk controller ROM. The last 128 KB are reserved for the ROM BIOS. Figure 2-1 shows how all this memory is allocated, using the traditional PC icon, the memory map.

The 640-KB DOS Barrier

As programs grew in size, and as new microprocessors that could access more memory were introduced, the limitations of the original PC design became apparent. Instead of being known as the point where program RAM stops and upper memory starts, 640 KB became known as the *DOS barrier*—a brick wall beyond which use of memory was forbidden.

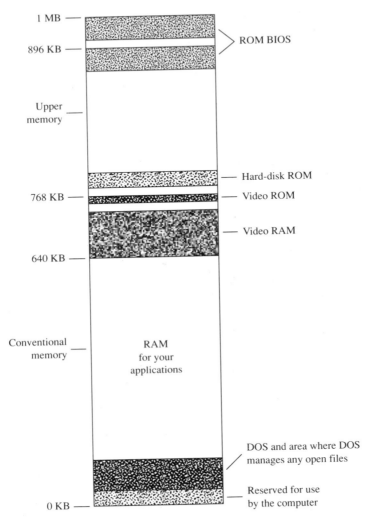

Figure 2-1. *The PC memory map.*

Programs could work only in the 640 KB (or less) of RAM that DOS gave them. In 1981, that was 10 times the amount available in any other microcomputer. But by the late 1980s, it was a pathetic amount of memory. Solutions were sought.

EXPANDED MEMORY

Spreadsheet users were the first to scream for more memory. While you're working on it, a spreadsheet is stored in memory; the more memory you have, the larger the spreadsheet you can generate. For the home budget, 256 KB was enough memory. For a small office, 640 KB was fine. But for Big Spreadsheet Users, it wasn't enough.

A solution was devised using a combination of both hardware and software. Lotus, Intel, and Microsoft devised the LIM expanded memory specification (EMS) standard for *expanded memory,* essentially a pool of extra memory in a PC. This isn't memory beyond the 1-MB mark, nor can programs run there. Instead, it's more like a memory storage area on an EMS-compatible expansion card inside the computer. EMS-compatible software could access the memory on the card, which in turn meant that the software could access more memory for storing data.

To use expanded memory on your computer, you need both an EMS-compatible memory expansion card and a device driver known as an *expanded memory manager* (EMM). You also need EMS-compatible applications that can use the expanded memory.

How Expanded Memory Works

Expanded memory takes advantage of an unused area of upper memory, reserving one 64-KB block of memory called the *page frame.* (See Figure 2-2.) The expanded memory sits by itself—away from the main memory in a PC—on an expansion card in one of the PC's expansion slots.

The EMM device driver makes expanded memory available to application software as four 16-KB pages mapped into the page frame. This memory is *bank-switched* by the hardware and software, meaning the 16-KB pages can be swapped in and out of the page frame as needed. As soon as it's in the page frame, a page can be accessed by the microprocessor because it falls within the 1-MB address space.

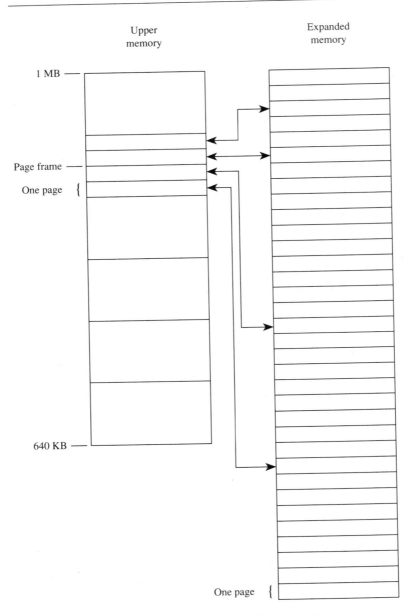

Figure 2-2. *How expanded memory is accessed.*

Using the functions provided by the EMM device driver, your applications can map other pages of expanded memory into the page frame. That's how expanded memory is used.

Note: EMS version 3.2 is really designed for storage, not for running programs. Mapping 16-KB pages of expanded memory into the page frame is fine for keeping unused portions of a spreadsheet in quick reach. But actual programs require contiguous memory directly accessible by the microprocessor.

The latest version of the EMS standard, version 4.0, provides access to as much as 32 MB of expanded memory. The EMS 4.0 standard allows newer EMS cards to move programs as well as data into expanded memory. As a result, expanded memory becomes more useful for multitasking, but it is still much slower than directly addressing conventional memory.

Using Backfill

In the early days, the PC came with 256 KB or less of installed memory on the motherboard. The only way to add memory was with a memory expansion card. With dropping memory prices, most computers today come with 640 KB or more.

An early function of the EMS expanded memory cards was to supply conventional memory in addition to expanded memory. The cards could be configured to give a 256-KB PC an extra 384 KB of conventional memory for a full 640 KB—and whatever memory was left over was configured as expanded memory. The process of filling in that conventional memory with expanded memory is known as *backfill*.

If your 8088, 8086, or 80286 computer already has 640 KB of conventional memory, you might consider disabling some of that memory. (This can usually be done with switches on the motherboard.) Then let a LIM EMS 4.0 expanded memory card fill in the disabled conventional memory with expanded memory.

This creates what is known as *mappable conventional memory*. This memory is like one huge page frame: The EMM device driver can swap all the backfill memory in and out of expanded memory. LIM EMS 4.0 theoretically lets the EMM device driver swap the entire 1-MB address range of the 8086 with expanded memory.

In practice, however, most EMS 4.0 memory boards are not fully compliant with the EMS 4.0 standard. For example, the Intel Above Board can only backfill conventional memory in the range 256 KB through 640 KB.

Note: The '386 microprocessor has powerful memory-mapping capabilities. Although 8088/8086 and 80286 systems require LIM EMS–compatible hardware and software, the '386 can simulate expanded memory in extended memory using an expanded memory emulator. This subject is covered in detail in Chapters 5 and 9.

EXTENDED MEMORY

What is extended memory? Basically, extended memory is RAM above and beyond the 1-MB mark on an 80286-based or '386-based PC. Remember: above and beyond. *Above* where DOS resides and *beyond* the reach of most DOS applications.

The 80286 can access up to 16 MB of RAM; the '386 can access up to 4096 MB. In all of those systems, previous versions of DOS treated the microprocessor like a fast 8088 with 1 MB of memory. Any memory above that 1-MB mark is referred to as *extended memory*. Figure 2-3 shows the memory map for a typical 80286-based or '386-based computer with extended memory.

The biggest problem with extended memory is that it's above the 8088's address space—therefore, DOS can't directly use extended memory. In order to use extended memory, a program must switch the microprocessor to protected mode and then switch back to real mode before quitting. The first programs to exploit this technique were RAM disks.

Because expanded memory was introduced before extended memory, more programs are designed to use expanded memory than extended memory. This is changing, however. AutoCAD and Lotus

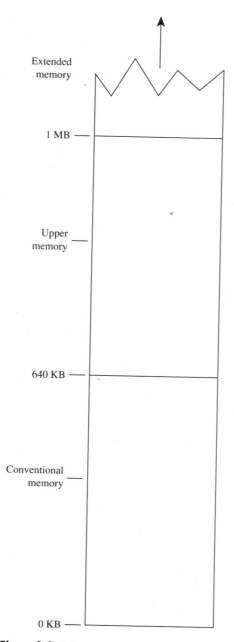

Figure 2-3. *The memory map for an 80286-based or '386-based computer with extended memory.*

1-2-3 version 3.0 can use extended memory. And Microsoft Windows in 386 enhanced mode opens the door to megabytes of extended memory.

Real and Protected Modes

To understand extended memory you must dive into the capabilities of the advanced 80286 and '386 microprocessors. These microprocessors actually have two modes of operation: *real mode* and *protected mode*.

- In real mode, the 80286 microprocessor operates just like an 8088; it can use only 1 MB of RAM, and extended memory can't be used for running programs.

- In protected mode, the 80286 cuts loose. It can access 16 MB of RAM and run programs anywhere. Extended memory is wide open for the microprocessor.

A '386 has real and protected modes, just like the 80286. In real mode, a '386 operates as a very fast 8088, but in protected mode a '386 can access up to 4096 MB of RAM for running programs and storing information. Additionally, when running an operating system that supports protected mode, a '386 has a mode called *virtual*

What Is Shadow RAM?

Shadow RAM is a technology that copies video and system BIOS into an unused area of RAM that is mapped into upper memory when the computer boots. Because RAM is faster than ROM, this enhances overall system performance. Like cache memory, shadow RAM can't be added to your computer—you must purchase a system that already has shadow RAM installed.

If you want to buy a computer with shadow RAM, be sure the shadow RAM can be disabled. Such a disable feature is important with some applications to resolve memory conflicts.

8086, or *V-86*, mode. In that mode, the operating system can run multiple programs. Each program believes it is running on a separate 8088 microprocessor with its own unique 1-MB address space. This is how DESQview 386 multitasks DOS applications.

Protected mode sounds like a RAM-hungry user's dream: lots of memory and the full power of the microprocessor to use it. Yet DOS is linked to the 8088; it's a real-mode-only operating system. DOS cannot run in protected mode, nor can it run programs in extended memory.

Using Extended Memory Under DOS

Although extended memory is really out of the DOS picture (for now), some potential exists:

- Some applications can run in—and will use—extended memory. These are the so-called *extended-DOS* applications. Secretly, these programs switch the microprocessor from real to protected mode—behind DOS's back. When the application runs, it's using the full power of the microprocessor and all the extended memory in the computer. When the application quits and returns to DOS, the application downshifts the microprocessor back into real mode. A few programs do this, most notably Windows, Lotus 1-2-3 versions 3.0 and later, and some versions of AutoCAD.

- Since DOS version 3.2, extended memory has been available for use as memory storage. You can place RAM disks, disk caches, or print buffers into extended memory. (This topic is covered in Chapter 7.) As long as programs aren't running in that memory, DOS can access it for storage purposes.

- Extended memory can simulate expanded memory—but only on '386-based computers and only with the proper software (an expanded memory emulator).

In order to accomplish these feats, Lotus, Intel, AST Research, and Microsoft established a standard for dealing with extended memory under DOS. It's the *Extended Memory Specification*, or XMS.

XMS doesn't allow programs to run in extended memory; you're still limited to the three functions described above. But XMS does establish the standards that provide sophisticated, cooperative use of extended memory under DOS.

DOS 5 SOLUTIONS

DOS 5 opens up new doors for using memory on a PC, especially 80286-based and '386-based systems. Along with those new opportunities come some new terms used to describe memory.

The High Memory Area

The 8088/8086 microprocessors can address 1 MB of memory. Any attempt to address memory beyond 1 MB causes the microprocessor to *wrap around*, back to memory location 0. (This works like the old Asteroids video game: When you flew your ship off the top of the screen, it reappeared at the bottom.)

The 80286 and '386 also wrap around to location 0. They can also map these bytes into the first 64 KB of extended memory. These extra 65,520 bytes are known as the *high memory area*, or HMA. Refer to Figure 2-4. Assume that the HMA provides DOS with an extra 64 KB of memory, even though the HMA is actually 16 bytes short of 64 KB.

That extra memory can be used by DOS on an 80286-based or '386-based computer. DOS can actually "see" the memory sitting up there and access it directly without having to switch the microprocessor into protected mode.

Why Not Write a Protected-Mode Version of DOS?

A protected-mode version of DOS does exist! It's called OS/2, and it uses the protected mode of the 80286 and extended memory. Of course, most people's needs are currently being met by less powerful PCs running DOS.

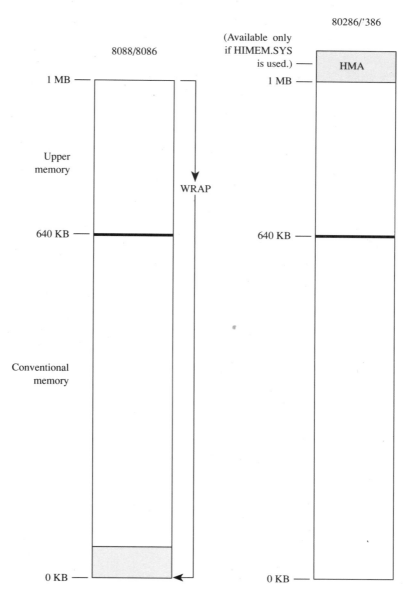

Figure 2-4. *How to fool DOS into seeing an extra 64 KB of memory.*

In order to access the HMA—an extra 64 KB of memory—you need
two things:

■ An 80286-based or '386-based PC with extended memory

■ A device driver to access and control the HMA

Most 80286-based and '386-based PCs come with 1 MB of RAM installed. The first 640 KB of that memory is conventional memory.
The rest is usually extended memory. (Note that some older AT computers come with only 512 KB of memory installed.) Therefore,
nearly all 80286-based or later computers have the extended memory
needed for DOS to access.

The device driver that accesses the HMA is HIMEM.SYS. Additionally, HIMEM.SYS implements the XMS standard on 80268-based
and '386-based computers running under DOS 5. It's the first step
toward taking full advantage of your computer's memory potential.

Upper Memory Blocks

Upper memory blocks (UMBs) are unused areas in upper memory.
Refer to Figure 2-5.

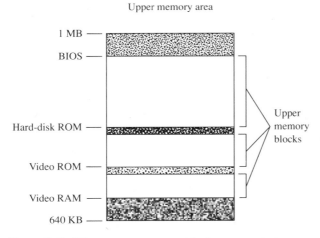

Figure 2-5. *Where upper memory blocks are created.*

Although IBM set aside 384 KB for ROM and future expansion, very little of it is used. The BIOS uses only part of the upper 128 KB of this memory; the hard-disk controller and video BIOS occupy only a sliver of the memory; and the video memory can take up anywhere from 4 KB (for monochrome) to 32 KB (for CGA) to 128 KB (for both EGA and VGA). As a result, there are unused portions of upper memory.

The unused areas between the various ROMs and other goodies in reserved memory cannot be used to run programs. Why? Because there is no actual RAM up there. RAM stops at 640 KB. (While it's true that video RAM is in reserved memory, it's designated for the video system, not for running programs.)

Before DOS 5, you needed to buy a third-party memory management program such as 386MAX from Qualitas or QEMM-386 from Quarterdeck if you wanted to create UMBs. These programs can map expanded memory into the unused areas between 640 KB and 1 MB. DOS 5 includes the necessary device drivers and programs to create UMBs on any '386-based computer that has at least 350 KB of extended memory. Creating UMBs is covered in detail in Chapters 5 and 9. The benefit? With device drivers and memory-resident software out of conventional memory, you have more conventional memory in which to run programs.

After you have the UMBs, you can do a number of things with them. For example, device drivers and memory-resident programs are typically placed into the UMBs. Although they're programs, they still run properly because they're still sitting in the 8088's 1-MB address space.

DOS 5 takes this concept one bold step further: You can transfer the DOS kernel (DOS's own resident programs) from conventional memory into the HMA, leaving you with oodles of conventional memory for running your applications.

CONCLUSION

All this information—all the new terms and different types of memory—requires a special section to wrap things up. To recap:

- Conventional memory is memory from 0 KB through 640 KB. It's where DOS runs programs. It's the only memory allocated in a PC for that purpose; DOS cannot run programs elsewhere.

- For DOS-based programs, expanded memory is the most important. Programs that want to access expanded memory can do so—but only for data-storage purposes. You cannot run programs in expanded memory.

- Extended memory is memory above 1 MB in an 80286-based or '386-based computer. DOS can use extended memory for data storage, but you cannot run DOS programs there. Programs written for Microsoft Windows can take full advantage of extended memory. In 386 enhanced mode, Windows can even use extended memory to simulate expanded memory.

- The memory benefits under DOS 5 are greater on 80286-based and '386-based computers. With those systems you can get an extra 64 KB of conventional memory by means of the high memory area (HMA).

- Using expanded memory and a third-party memory manager, you can fill in unused areas of upper memory to create upper memory blocks (UMBs). DOS 5 can create UMBs on a '386-based computer with at least 350 KB of extended memory. Into those blocks you can transfer your device drivers and memory-resident software, freeing up that much-needed conventional memory.

SUMMARY

Memory in a PC is a confusing issue; a variety of terms are used to describe the types of and locations for the computer's memory. There's no skirting around this: You must understand the terms in order to get the most from your computer's memory. Here are the most important concepts:

■ All computers have RAM and ROM: RAM stores information; ROM contains information that can be read by the microprocessor but cannot be changed.

■ The original PC's 1-MB address space was divided into 640 KB for RAM and 384 KB for ROM and future expansion.

■ Because 640 KB wasn't enough memory for some applications, Lotus, Intel, and Microsoft developed the LIM Expanded Memory Specification. This allowed EMS-compatible applications to access 8 MB of expanded memory, although that memory could be used only for storage, not for running programs.

■ The EMS standard is the hardware and software specification for expanded memory.

■ Memory above 1 MB on an 80286-based or '386-based computer is called extended memory. DOS cannot run programs in extended memory. Extended memory can, however, be used by some special applications and for data storage.

■ The XMS defines a software interface that enables 80286-based and '386-based computers to use extended memory.

■ The high memory area (HMA) is the first 64-KB segment of extended memory on 80286-based and '386-based computers with extended memory. DOS 5 takes direct advantage of the HMA.

■ Upper memory blocks (UMBs) are unused areas of upper memory that have been filled with RAM. On '386-based computers with 350 KB of extended memory, DOS 5 maps extended memory into unused areas in upper memory to create the UMBs. Third-party memory managers create UMBs by mapping expanded memory into unused areas in upper memory. When filled with RAM, the UMBs can be used to store device drivers and memory-resident programs.

Chapter 3

Peeking at Memory

Curiosity can be a passion or a passing fancy. Some people want to take a piano apart and see how it works, whereas others simply want to play it. DOS 5 provides you with two commands—Debug and Mem—that let you examine memory to the degree necessary to satisfy your curiosity.

USING DEBUG

Debug is dynamite in a baby buggy; it's both powerful and simple. Using Debug, you can look at memory; manipulate memory; write small programs in memory; and load portions of disk into memory, change them, and save them back. We'll be using Debug to examine memory; it's beyond the scope of this book to get into writing programs or changing portions of memory.

1. At the DOS prompt, type the Debug command and press Enter. The Debug prompt—a hyphen—will appear:

```
C:\>debug
-
```

   (If you get the message *Bad command or file name*, change to your DOS directory and type the command again.)

2. To list the commands that are part of the Debug utility, type a question mark and press Enter. Figure 3-1 shows the result.

```
assemble      A [address]
compare       C range address
dump          D [range]
enter         E address [list]
fill          F range list
go            G [=address] [addresses]
hex           H value1 value2
input         I port
load          L [address] [drive] [firstsector] [number]
move          M range address
name          N [pathname] [arglist]
output        O port byte
proceed       P [=address] [number]
quit          Q
register      R [register]
search        S range list
trace         T [=address] [value]
unassemble    U [range]
write         W [address] [drive] [firstsector] [number]
allocate expanded memory        XA [#pages]
deallocate expanded memory      XD [handle]
map expanded memory pages       XM [Lpage] [Ppage] [handle]
display expanded memory status  XS
```

Figure 3-1. *Debug's Help command output.*

Looking at Memory with the Dump Command

The Dump command is the true memory voyeur: It displays the raw contents of memory on a byte-by-byte basis. To use the Dump command, type *d* and then press Enter. You will see 128 bytes of the PC's memory, arranged as shown in Figure 3-2. (Your values will be different.)

Memory address	Values of the 16 bytes at each memory address	ASCII equivalents of the 16 bytes

```
4C01:0100  20 20 2E 94 13 92 A4 C6-B1 E2 12 45 45 83 90 07    .........EE...
4C01:0110  00 72 DC 3D 08 00 76 50-EB D5 83 7E 08 20 73 06    .r.=..uP...~. s.
4C01:0120  B8 4B 08 E9 84 00 FF 76-0E FF 76 0C FF 76 0A 0E    .K.....u..u..u..
4C01:0130  2A 20 30 32 6A 72 2E 2E-2E 5A 6F 6F 6D 21 20 2A    * 02jr...Zoom! *
4C01:0140  0E E8 C4 09 83 C4 04 89-46 FE 0B C0 75 34 FF 76    ........F...u4.u
4C01:0150  16 FF 76 14 0E E8 60 0C-83 C4 04 89 46 FE 0B C0    ..u...`.....F...
4C01:0160  75 20 B8 3A 08 EB 43 90-FF 76 0C FF 76 0A 8B 46    u .:..C..u..u..F
4C01:0170  08 48 50 2B C0 50 9A 16-89 AB 33 0B C0 75 BB E9    .HP+.P....3..u..
```

Figure 3-2. *The Dump command displays 128 bytes of memory.*

Each line of the Dump command's output displays 16 bytes—one paragraph—of memory. The display is broken into three columns:

- The first column displays the address of the first byte.

- The second column displays the 16 bytes of memory starting from the address shown in the first column.

■ The third column displays the ASCII characters that corre-
spond to those 16 bytes.

Bytes that have no corresponding ASCII character are displayed as
periods. The memory addresses and the byte values are displayed in
hexadecimal.

Although the Debug information is intended for programmers, with
patience you can discover the secrets that memory holds.

Type the following Dump command and press Enter:

```
-d 40:0
```

Debug will display 128 bytes of a low memory area officially known
as the *BIOS data area.*

Hidden among these bytes is the amount of memory in your computer, the number of disk drives you have, the keyboard buffer (an
area where keystrokes are saved), the video mode, and the current
time. Of course, this information is in hexadecimal and is not very
obvious.

Getting a Handle on Hex

Debug uses *hexadecimal* (base-16) numbers. (Hexadecimal is
often shortened to simply hex.) Each hexadecimal digit represents a number from 0 through 15. Hexadecimal digits are
identical to decimal digits from 0 through 9, and the letters A
through F represent the numbers 10 through 15.

The numbers that Debug displays are all two-digit hexadecimal numbers, so they're relatively easy to translate to decimal—multiply the left digit by 16 and add the right digit. You
will get a value from 0 through 255. For example, the hexadecimal number A3 is decimal 163 ($10 \times 16 + 3$). The hexadecimal
number FF is decimal 255 ($15 \times 16 + 15$).

Now type the following command and press Enter:

```
-d fe00:0
```

Debug will display 128 bytes in the upper memory—in ROM. Specifically, this is the location of your computer's BIOS. You might see your BIOS's copyright notice as it's stored in ROM.

Changing Memory

As a memory tool, Debug lets you look at and access memory anywhere DOS can look at and access memory. You can even change memory, although this isn't something you should do casually.

A good place you can change memory is in video memory. Any changes you make there appear on the display for immediate feedback. Type the following Fill command and press Enter:

```
-f b800:0 FA0 21 ce
```

This command tells Debug to fill FA0 (4000 decimal) bytes starting at location B800:0000 (use B000:0000 on computers with monochrome monitors) with the byte pattern 21 CE. This command changes the background color to red and causes blinking yellow exclamation points to fill the screen. Why does this happen?

Address B800:0000 (B000:0000 on computers with monochrome monitors) is the start of video memory. An 80-column text screen (80 columns × 25 rows) has 2000 characters. However, it takes 2 bytes to store a screen character in memory. The first byte is the character's ASCII value—literally, the character to be displayed; the second byte is the character's screen *attribute*. (This byte controls the character's color and intensity and whether the character should blink.) Therefore, an 80-column text screen is 4000 (FA0 hex) bytes long.

The ASCII character for hex 21 is an exclamation point. Screen attribute CE is a blinking character, with a yellow foreground on a red background. So this command fills the screen with blinking yellow exclamation points on a red background.

You can verify this by typing the following Dump command. (If you have a monochrome monitor, change *b800* to *b000*.)

```
-d b800:0
```

You will see 128 bytes containing the pattern 21 CE repeated over and over.

To return to a normal screen, exit Debug by typing *q* and pressing Enter. Clear the screen by typing *CLS* and pressing Enter.

Examining Expanded Memory

If you have expanded memory installed, the DOS 5 version of Debug will let you work with it just as you can work with conventional and upper memory. Most of the commands that access expanded memory (the *X* commands) deal with advanced memory concepts beyond the scope of our present investigation. However, the XS command lets you display the status of your expanded memory driver. Run Debug again, type the following command, and press Enter:

```
-xs
```

Provided you have expanded memory in your computer, you will see a display similar to this:

```
Handle xxxx has xxxx page allocated
Physical page xx = Frame segment xxxx
Physical page xx = Frame segment xxxx
...
  xx of a total  xxx EMS pages have been allocated
  xx of a total  xxx EMS handles have been allocated
```

The xx's will be actual values. If you don't have any expanded memory, Debug responds with the message *EMS not installed*. This is all interesting and fun. But Debug falls short on being informative—it doesn't tell you what you're looking at. It could be data stored in memory, a memory-resident program, a device driver, DOS, or just some unused part of memory.

To quit Debug, type *q* and press Enter.

Note: *If you're interested in exploring your PC's memory, check out* The *New* Peter Norton Programmer's Guide to the IBM PC & PS/2 *(Microsoft Press, 1988).*

USING MEM

Whereas Debug displays the contents of memory, the Mem command tells you what programs and device drivers are in memory. The Mem command was introduced with DOS 4—the first version of DOS that actively supported both extended and expanded memory.

On the surface, the Mem command simply reports available memory. Typing the Mem command without any options yields a brief summary of how memory is used in your computer:

```
C:\>mem
    655360 bytes total conventional memory
    655360 bytes available to MS-DOS
    637600 largest executable program size
```

If any expanded or extended memory is available, the Mem command reports the total amount in the computer, plus how much is available (not being used).

Obviously, greed is the key here. The more memory you have available, the more you can do with it. But it's not simply a question of having 640 KB of conventional memory and 2 MB of extended memory. The issue is *how much of that memory you can use*. In the preceding example, the largest executable program size is 637 KB—quite a bit, thanks to DOS 5. That value can grow even greater, which is the point of this whole book.

The /Program, /Debug, and /Classify Switches

The Mem command has three optional switches:

■ The /program switch provides a list of all programs, system data areas, and installed device drivers in memory, their locations and sizes (in both decimal and hexadecimal), and the total amount of conventional, expanded, and extended memory in your computer, plus the available amount of each.

■ The /debug switch provides the same information but also displays system and device drivers (such as the printer and the clock).

- The /classify switch provides a list of the names and sizes of all programs in memory.

The output from the Mem command when used with an optional switch is quite long. It's best to use the pipe character—the broken vertical line (¦)—and the More filter when issuing the Mem command in that manner. Type the following:

```
C:\>mem /program ¦ more
```

Press Enter, and you'll see the first screen of information listing programs and installed device drivers in memory. (See Figure 3-3.) The four columns on the display tell you the location (address) of every program or device driver in memory, the name of the program or

```
Address     Name        Size      Type
-------     ---------   -------   -------
000000                  000400    Interrupt Vector
000400                  000100    ROM Communication Area
000500                  000200    DOS Communication Area

000700      IO          000A60    System Data

001160      MSDOS       00A410    System Data

00B570      IO          003BE0    System Data
                        000820     FILES=
                        000100     FCBS=
                        002990     BUFFERS=
                        0008F0     LASTDRIVE=
00F160      COMMAND     001160    Program
0102D0      MSDOS       000040    -- Free --
010320      COMMAND     0001B0    Environment
0104E0      MSDOS       0000C0    -- Free --
0105B0      MOUSE       003A80    Program
014040      DOSKEY      000F30    Program
014F80      MEM         0000D0    Environment
```

```
015060      MSDOS       001230    -- Free --
0162B0      MEM         0176F0    Program
02D9B0      MSDOS       072640    -- Free --


   655360 bytes total conventional memory
   655360 bytes available to MS-DOS
   569200 largest executable program size

  7340032 bytes total contiguous extended memory
  7340032 bytes available contiguous extended memory
```

Figure 3-3. *The output of Mem /program.*

device driver, its size in bytes (in hexadecimal), and the memory type (what the memory is being used for—to store a program or a device driver, for example). Press the spacebar to display another screen of information. The last screen will show the amount of conventional, expanded, and extended memory in your computer, plus the available amount of each.

The /debug switch provides the same information as the /program switch but displays system device drivers as well.

Only programmers and network administrators will need to use all the information produced by the output of *mem /debug*. Some of the information, however, is important to all DOS 5 users. The new /classify switch was added to display this information.

The output from Mem and its optional switches is all interesting and curious. However, it wasn't until DOS 5 that the Mem command really became useful. Under DOS 5, you can transfer some of the listed programs and device drivers from conventional memory into upper memory, specifically into the upper memory blocks. (This is covered in Chapters 5 and 6.)

Without the /classify switch, you'd have had to hunt down the programs in the output of the Mem /program command, ferret out the size of the programs in hexadecimal, do some math, pull out a clump of hair, and then use the proper DOS 5 commands to relocate the program. The /classify switch was devised to make that operation easier on you—and your hair.

The output from the Mem /classify command is still quite long, so type the following and press Enter:

```
C:\>mem /classify ¦ more
```

You will see a display something like the one shown in Figure 3-4.

The display now shows you which programs are in conventional memory and how much space each program occupies. The other technical information isn't cluttering up the display.

```
Conventional Memory :

   Name            Size in Decimal        Size in Hex
--------------     ----------------      --------------
   MSDOS              61712    ( 60.3K)       F110
   COMMAND             4880    (  4.8K)       1310
   MOUSE              14976    ( 14.6K)       3A80
   DOSKEY              3888    (  3.8K)       F30
   FREE                  64    (  0.1K)       40
   FREE                 192    (  0.2K)       C0
   FREE                 224    (  0.2K)       E0
   FREE              569200    (555.8K)      8AF70

Total  FREE :        569680    (556.3K)

Total bytes available to programs :              569680    (556.3K)
Largest executable program size :                569200    (555.8K)

    7340032 bytes total contiguous extended memory
    7340032 bytes available contiguous extended memory
```

Figure 3-4. *The output of Mem /classify.*

In Figure 3-4, you see four programs and four FREE areas. The four programs are MSDOS, which occupies 60.3 KB; COMMAND (actually, COMMAND.COM), occupying 4.8 KB; the mouse device driver, using 14.6 KB; and the memory-resident program DOSKEY, using 3.8 KB. The FREE memory areas total some 556.3 KB, all of which is available to DOS.

But what's important for DOS 5 are the programs listed in memory. If you move MSDOS and DOSKEY to upper memory blocks, you'll have 88 KB more conventional memory.

Mem Command Tips

■ The /program and /debug switches can be abbreviated as /p and /d. The /classify switch can be abbreviated as /c.

■ Piping the output of the Mem command through the More filter will pause the display, but often you need a hard copy. To obtain one, type the following command and press Enter:

```
C:\>mem /c > prn
```

Press the Form Feed button on your printer to eject the page. Substitute /p or /d for /c as needed.

Removing MSDOS from conventional memory is easy under DOS 5. But to determine if you can relocate the mouse device driver and DOSKEY into an upper memory block, you need to know how big the mouse device driver and DOSKEY are. And that's where the /classify switch comes in handy.

Other Mem Command Information

The Mem command tells you how much conventional, expanded, and extended memory your computer has and how much of each is available. If you specify an optional switch, the Mem command also tells you what programs and device drivers are in memory, where each is located, and how much memory each occupies. The Mem command also reports on two additional items if they're available: the *high memory area* (HMA) and the *upper memory blocks* (UMBs).

The HMA is the first 64 KB of extended memory on 80286-based and '386-based computers with extended memory. When an extended memory manager, such as the HIMEM.SYS device driver that comes with DOS 5, is installed, DOS can access the HMA. Part of DOS (the MSDOS program) can be transferred to the HMA, freeing precious conventional memory.

If you own an 80286-based or '386-based computer with extended memory and have installed an extended memory manager, the last line of any Mem command will be

```
64Kb High Memory Area available
```

(In this message, DOS 5 uses Kb to denote kilobytes.)

If DOS has been transferred to the HMA, the Mem command reports

```
MS-DOS resident in High Memory Area
```

If anything else is using the HMA, you'll see

```
High Memory Area in use
```

And if DOS is on a ROM chip in your computer, you'll see

```
MS-DOS resident in ROM using High Memory Area
```

When you create UMBs for storing device drivers and memory-resident programs, they're reported in the output of the Mem /classify command. This is shown in Figure 3-5.

The Mem /classify command now shows you information about the UMBs, what programs are loaded into UMBs (the mouse driver and DOSKEY in Figure 3-5), and how much free memory is available. The total memory available to programs now reflects memory available in both conventional and upper memory. The commands described in Chapters 5, 6, and 9 let you take advantage of this memory under DOS 5.

```
Conventional Memory :

   Name              Size in Decimal        Size in Hex
   ------------      ------------------      --------------
   MSDOS             14736    ( 14.4K)          3990
   HIMEM             1184     (  1.2K)          4A0
   EMM386            8400     (  8.2K)          20D0
   COMMAND           2800     (  2.7K)          AF0
   FREE              64       (  0.1K)          40
   FREE              224      (  0.2K)          E0
   FREE              627728   (608.5K)          99410

Total  FREE :       628016   (613.2K)

Upper Memory :

   Name              Size in Decimal        Size in Hex
   ------------      ------------------      --------------
   SYSTEM            163840   (160.0K)          28000
   MOUSE             14976    ( 14.6K)          3A80
   DOSKEY            3888     (  3.8K)          F30
```

```
   FREE              192      (  0.2K)
   FREE              46400    ( 45.3K)          B540

Total  FREE :       46592    ( 45.5K)

Total bytes available to programs (Conventional+Upper) :      674608   (658.7K)
Largest executable program size :                            628016   (613.2K)
Largest available upper memory block :                        46400   ( 45.3K)

   7340032 bytes total contiguous extended memory
         0 bytes available contiguous extended memory
   7121920 bytes available XMS memory
           MS-DOS resident in High Memory Area
```

Figure 3-5. *Mem /classify after establishing UMBs.*

SUMMARY

Two DOS tools let you look at memory: the Debug utility and the Mem command. Metaphorically speaking, the Mem command is for those who want to play the piano; Debug is for those who want to take the piano apart.

■ Debug lets you examine or change memory, create small programs, load sections of disk into memory, save memory to disk, and perform other miscellaneous (and powerful) functions.

■ Debug lets you look at bytes stored at memory addresses. (These bytes are listed in hexadecimal.)

■ The Mem command tells you the total and available amounts of conventional, expanded, and extended memory in your computer.

■ The Mem command's optional /program switch displays a summary of all programs and device drivers in memory and their locations, sizes, and types. The /debug switch produces the same summary but also displays system device drivers.

■ The Mem command's /classify switch tells you—in an easy-to-read format—which programs are loaded into memory and how much memory they occupy. This information is helpful in transferring device drivers and memory-resident programs into upper memory blocks.

Chapter 4

Adding Memory to Your System

To take full advantage of the memory potential of your PC, you might have to install additional memory chips in your computer. In this chapter, you'll learn all about memory chips: the obscure jargon that surrounds them, the shopping strategies that help you make a wise purchase, and the installation instructions that put them to good use.

ABOUT RAM CHIPS

Until you get to know them, it's perfectly okay to say that all RAM chips look alike. From a distance, they do. You could spend a slow weekend plugging them into the drywall in the guest bathroom for an incredibly interesting (albeit expensive) tile effect. Yet, upon closer examination, your visitors would notice that each chip has different markings on top.

Those markings on the top of a RAM chip are, in essence, your only clue to the chip's identity. As we saw in Chapter 1, a RAM chip is rated according to its *capacity* and *speed*:

- A RAM chip's capacity reflects how many bits it holds. (That's bits—not bytes.) Typical RAM chips store 64 Kb, 256 Kb, and 1 Mb. Because it takes nine of these chips to make up one bank, in the end you do wind up with a full 64 KB, 256 KB, or 1 MB of memory.

- A RAM chip's speed is measured in *nanoseconds* (ns), or one-billionth of a second—the time it takes a beam of light to travel about one foot. Slow RAM chips operate at 150 ns, medium-pokey RAM chips from 120 to 100 ns, and fast RAM chips at 80 ns and below.

When you buy RAM chips, you buy them nine to a bank. Since most RAM chips are measured by the bit, that's eight chips for the 8 bits in a byte, plus one chip for a parity bit.

DIPs, SIMMs, and SIPs

RAM chips come in several different styles: DIPs, which are individual RAM chips; SIMMs, which contain one bank of RAM in a single handy package; and SIPs, which can be individual chips or multiple chips in a single package.

- DIP stands for *Dual In-line Package*. This is the most common type of chip: a flat rectangle, usually with 16 metal legs evenly divided between the right and left sides, as shown in Figure 4-1.

Figure 4-1. *A DIP.*

DIPs plug into little sockets—much as Lego bricks fit together. But unlike a Lego brick, a DIP can be easily damaged—or even inserted in the wrong direction—while being plugged in.

- SIMMs are a revolutionary concept for upgrading memory. SIMM stands for *Single In-line Memory Module*. Basically, a SIMM is a tiny expansion card, about half the size of a pocket comb, as shown in Figure 4-2. Nine RAM chips—an entire bank of RAM—are soldered to the card. To install a SIMM, you simply plug in the entire SIMM card, gliding its edge connector into a SIMM socket (with the power off, of course).

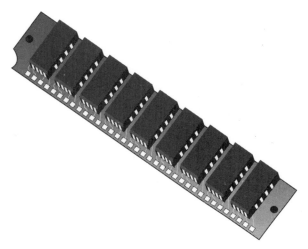

Figure 4-2. *A SIMM.*

■ Another style of RAM chip is the SIP. A SIP (*Single In-line Package*) looks like a moustache comb, as shown in Figure 4-3. Instead of having an edge connector (like a SIMM), a SIP has rows of tiny metal legs, which you plug into corresponding rows of tiny holes. Although a SIP—like a SIMM—contains a

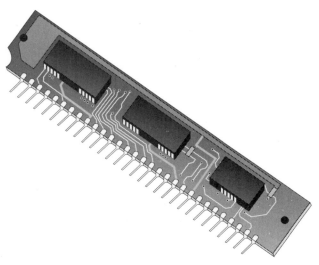

Figure 4-3. *A SIP.*

full bank of memory, its legs make it much more susceptible to damage. Accordingly, SIPs are less popular than SIMMs.

Identifying a RAM Chip

All RAM chips, whether DIPs, SIMMs, or SIPs, have markings on top. These markings provide the following information about the RAM chip:

- Its manufacturer. A company's logo or initials generally appear somewhere on the chip.

- Its capacity. A number such as 1256 identifies a 256-Kb chip; 11000 or 1100 means a 1-Mb chip. Chances are that if a chip has the number 256 or 100, it's a 256-Kb or a 1-Mb chip.

- Its speed. This value usually appears immediately after the capacity. A dash typically separates the two. Speed values are -15 for 150 ns, -12 for 120 ns, -10 for 100 ns, -80 for 80 ns, -70 for 70 ns, and so on.

- Its proper socket orientation, noted by a notch or a dot on the chip. The notch should match a similar notch or dot on the chip's socket. If you install a DIP, you must pay close attention to the notch in order to properly orient the chip before plugging it in. (See Figure 4-6.)

Lots of mysterious (and unimportant) numbers can appear on a chip. For example, consider the chip depicted in Figure 4-4.

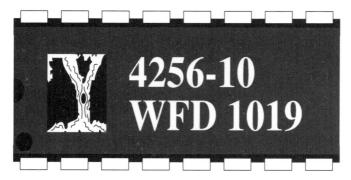

Figure 4-4. *A typical RAM chip.*

This chip comes from the Hollow Tree Manufacturing Company, as seen by the distinctive logo. It's a 256-Kb chip rated at 100 ns. Note the dot and the notch. That's the important information; the rest of the information is of use primarily to the manufacturer.

If you encounter a chip you cannot identify, take a guess. The number 1259 probably indicates a 256-Kb chip, with the 9 stuck in there for some unknown reason.

SHOPPING FOR MEMORY

About the best advice I can give for buying memory chips is the following:

1. **Know how much memory you need.** If you want to upgrade a PC from 256 KB to 640 KB of memory, you need 384 KB of chips—that's simple math. If you're adding expanded memory, find out how much memory your software needs. Also, you should be aware of the type of memory chips your PC needs. Your PC's motherboard might need one bank of 256-Kb chips and two banks of 64-Kb chips—or maybe even some unusual 128x4-bit chips. (Few computers require this type of chip.) Some expanded memory cards accept upgrades only in 512-KB increments (two banks of 256-Kb chips); some '386-based systems let you upgrade only 1, 2, or 4 MB at a time. Check your computer's manual.

2. **Figure out the number and capacity of the chips you need.** This again is simple math, but it also requires a knowledge of what you're upgrading. If the hardware requires DIPs and you need 512 KB, that's two banks of 256-Kb RAM chips, or eighteen chips. A 1-MB memory upgrade might require only one 1-MB SIMM. However, depending on your hardware requirements, your computer might need nine 1-Mb DIP chips or thirty-six 256-Kb DIP chips instead.

Note: Usually all memory banks must have chips of the same capacity. You can't add two banks of 1-MB chips to two banks of 256-KB chips and expect to have another 2 MB of RAM. See your computer's manual for details on the proper chip capacity.

3. **Know the speed of the chips.** The speed of the chips is totally hardware dependent; the faster your microprocessor, the faster (and more expensive) the chips you need.

Note: The chip speed listed in your computer's manual is usually the optimum desired speed. If you plug in slower chips, you simply degrade the PC's performance slightly. You can even mix chips of different speeds within the same bank. The only drawback is that the memory bank operates at the speed of the slowest chip— possibly adding a wait state to the computer. My advice: Don't be cheap. Buy the faster chips.

The manual for your computer or expansion card describes the number, type, capacity, and speed of the chips you need to buy.

Understanding a Memory Ad

To be a shrewd shopper, you must be educated in the subtleties of reading memory ads. Consider the ad from Mondo Pete's Memory Emporium, as shown in Figure 4-5.

In Mondo Pete's ad, 1-Mb and 256-Kb DIPs are listed first, each according to its speed. A 256x1-80ns is a 256-Kb chip with an 80-nanosecond access time. Next come 1-MB SIMMs, also listed by speed. With SIMMs you need to be careful: Macintosh computers use SIMMs exactly like PCs do, but the Mac SIMMs contain only eight chips. Most ads use ''x8'' to identify Mac SIMMs and ''x9'' to identify PC SIMMs. Therefore, a 1Mbx9-80 SIMM is an 80-nanosecond, 1-MB PC SIMM.

A memory upgrade kit is another option. Some memory merchants sell chips bundled as memory upgrade kits. If your computer is listed, then you can buy the corresponding memory upgrade kit, which might be nothing more than four SIMMs rubber-banded together, plus photocopied instructions.

Figure 4-5. *Mondo Pete's Memory Emporium.*

Normally all chip prices will be listed. Remember that if you're buying DIPs, you need nine chips altogether, so multiply the price by nine. $CALL means ''The price on this chip changes frequently, so call for the current price.''

Because memory merchants deal with memory full time, they're usually more open to questions than other over-the-phone hardware dealers. If your computer's manual recommends a certain type of chip, ask the dealer whether it's in stock.

One suggestion: Try to get all chips of the same brand. This applies directly to DIPs. As you verify the capacity and speed on the chips, be sure they're all of the same brand. There's less chance of problems occurring if all the chips come from the same manufacturer.

Buy chips from places that will accept returns. Occasionally, a bad chip appears. It's nice to be able to get a replacement.

And there's nothing wrong with shipping memory through the mail; most memory comes in static-free tubes. As long as your over-zealous letter carrier doesn't bend and stuff the tube into your mailbox, you'll be okay.

You can also purchase memory from the dealer who sold you your PC. If you're timid about adding the memory, he or she will probably even add the memory for you—but probably not for free.

PUTTING MEMORY IN A PC

The act of adding memory to your system is tinker-toy simple. You need only know which kind of chips your PC needs.

Note: *The process of upgrading and fine-tuning DOS 5 for different types of computers is described in Chapter 10. The following information is simply general memory upgrading advice.*

8088/8086 Systems

You can add only conventional or expanded memory to an 8088-based or 8086-based PC: These microprocessors cannot use extended memory. If you already have 640 KB of conventional memory, your only option is to buy an expanded memory card. My advice is to buy a LIM EMS 4.0–compatible expanded memory card, regardless of how much conventional memory you already have. Fill the expanded memory card with as much memory as you can afford—at least 512 KB, but preferably 1 MB or more.

Next follow the instructions that came with the board to backfill as much conventional memory with expanded memory as possible, to create mappable conventional memory. You might need to disable some of your computer's conventional memory. This is done by changing switches on your computer's motherboard. (Consult your computer's manual for the location and the proper setting of these switches.) Configure any unused memory on the expansion card as expanded memory.

If expanded memory cards are out of your price range, your priority is to pack your motherboard full of conventional memory. Some older systems could accept only 256 KB on the motherboard; the other 384 KB had to be supplied on memory expansion cards. See the dealer you bought your PC from for such a card.

80286 Systems

An 80286-based PC can use conventional memory, extended memory, and expanded memory.

Most 80286-based PCs have sockets so that 1 to 8 MB (or more) of memory can be installed directly on the motherboard. The first 640 KB of this is conventional memory; the rest is extended memory. An 80286-based PC with 1 MB of memory on the motherboard has 640 KB of conventional memory and 384 KB of extended memory.

My advice is to use as little motherboard memory as possible. Disable all but 256 KB of your computer's conventional memory. Flip whatever switches tell the system that it has only 256 KB installed.

Next buy a LIM EMS 4.0–compatible expanded memory card. Pack that card full of RAM—at least 1 MB. Follow the instructions in the card's manual to configure half of the card's memory as expanded, the rest as extended. Then backfill the conventional memory that resides between 256 KB and 640 KB with expanded memory. (This creates mappable conventional memory that acts as one large page frame.)

Choosing an expanded memory board

Chances are that an 8088/8086/80286 solution involves adding expanded memory to your system. That means you'll need to purchase a LIM EMS 4.0–compatible expanded memory card.

Many expanded memory cards are available. The two most popular are AST's Rampage and Intel's Above Board. No matter which system you choose, be sure the card is LIM EMS 4.0 compatible.

As for the special options available on some expanded memory cards (serial port, printer port, clock, game port, and so on), buy them only if you need them.

Adding memory to an expanded memory card is easy, primarily because you can (and should) add memory to the card when it's out of the computer. This is easier than adding memory to a motherboard (which makes you feel like a RAM-chip dentist). Note that some expanded memory cards require upgrades in specific increments of RAM (256 KB, 512 KB, 1 MB, and so on).

LIM EMS 4.0 allows up to 32 MB of expanded memory. Some expanded memory cards can hold only 2 MB, with room for another 6 MB on a special *piggyback card*, which costs extra. You'll need four of these expanded memory cards (with piggyback cards as well) in your system to get the full 32 MB.

'386 Systems

Users with '386-based systems have the best hardware for taking advantage of memory. Here the advice is easy: Buy as much memory as you can afford. Some '386-based systems will even run faster as you add more memory. My recommendation is 4 MB of memory, minimum. All of that memory will be used as extended memory in the system. Later you'll see how to emulate expanded memory with extended memory by using EMM386.EXE (DOS's expanded memory emulator) or third-party memory-management software.

When adding memory to a '386-based system, be sure you use the special 32-bit memory upgrade slot. (The better systems will have these.) Avoid adding a memory expansion card designed for an 80286-based system; these cards "talk" to the microprocessor only 16 bits at a time, rather than the optimal 32 bits at a time.

Plugging in Chips

If you're going to add the memory, give yourself plenty of work space and good lighting. Get several sizes of Phillips and flathead screwdrivers and a needlenose pliers. Next turn your computer off, unplug it, and open the computer's case. (Refer to Chapter 1.) You will be inserting chips into either the computer's motherboard or a memory expansion card. If you're inserting chips into a memory expansion card, remember to do so *before* you insert the card into an expansion slot in the computer.

Note: Before you remove any cards from the computer or insert any chips, be sure you've discharged any static electricity you've built up. (Static electricity can actually fry a delicate memory chip.) Touch something metal, such as the computer's case or power supply, before touching any chips or cards. Try not to shuffle your feet in the carpet or pet a long-haired cat while you work. Also, do not touch the metal legs on a DIP or a SIP or the metal edge connector on a SIMM.

Installing DIPs

To install a DIP, follow these steps:

1. Slide one chip out of the tube.

2. Orient the chip so that the dot or notch is lined up with the notch on the first socket on the motherboard or memory expansion card. (See Figure 4-6.)

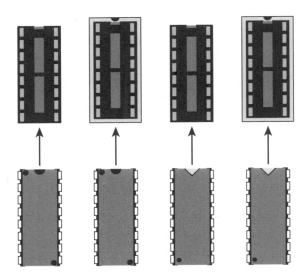

Figure 4-6. *Installing a chip in its socket.*

3. Set the chip down on top of the socket.

4. Carefully make sure every leg on the chip is lined up with its corresponding hole in the socket. You might need to remove the chip and gently bend one or more of the legs to ensure a proper fit. (A needlenose pliers is handy for this.)

5. When you're absolutely certain each leg is lined up with the proper hole, press down firmly but gently on the chip until you feel it seat.

Note: Most chips are bowlegged. You might need to lay the chip down on its side, bending the legs slightly inward so that they line up with the holes in the socket. Use a flat, wooden object for this. (A Popsicle stick is perfect.) Avoid touching the legs with your fingers.

Always work on one bank at a time in an orderly fashion. Take chips out of the tube one at a time. A wooden surface is best to work on because it doesn't conduct electricity.

When you've finished, inspect your work. Be sure that each chip is properly seated and that all the little legs are in the holes in the sockets. Sometimes one of the legs might bend out and away from its hole. You can remove the chip by alternately working a small flathead screwdriver gently under each end of the chip. Next straighten the leg with the needlenose pliers, and try to insert the chip again. (If this concerns you, buy a chip-insertion tool at an electronics store to make the job easier.) Note that the legs are fragile and can be bent only so many times before they break.

Installing SIMMs

SIMMs are much easier to install than DIPs. Follow these steps:

1. Slide one SIMM out of the tube.

2. Orient the SIMM so that the metal edge connector is above the slot. The SIMM faces chip-side away from the hook on each side of the slot.

3. Insert the SIMM at an angle into the slot on the motherboard or memory expansion card.

4. After the edge of the SIMM is in the slot, rotate the SIMM up until you hear it click into place. The hook on each side of the slot will pop into the hole on each side of the SIMM.

There is only one proper way to insert a SIMM, so if it doesn't seem to fit, flip it around and try again.

If you're installing chips on an expansion card, plug the expansion card into an expansion slot in the computer when you've finished. After installing new memory, you'll probably need to set some switches on the memory card or on your motherboard to tell the computer about the new memory. Most PCs require that you manually inform them of the amount of memory in the PC. Check the manuals that came with your computer and the memory expansion card for the precise location and settings of the switches.

Leave your computer's cover off for now—you want to be sure the new memory works before you screw the cover screws back in. Connect the power cord, monitor, and keyboard, though—you'll need them to test the memory.

The Obligatory Error Message

If you've added extended memory to an 80286-based or '386-based
system, you'll see a memory error message the next time the computer boots. This is because the computer "remembers" how much
memory was installed before you added the new memory. Turn your
computer on now, and ignore the memory error message. Run your
computer's Setup program to tell the computer about the newly installed memory, and the computer will "remember" the new
amount. You won't see the memory error message the next time the
computer boots. Note that 8088/8086-based systems don't get the
memory error message—these computers simply count up the
memory.

You might see the dreaded *Parity error* message. This usually means
there's a bad chip installed somewhere. Tracking it down can be
tough, unless it's improperly inserted or missing a leg in a socket.
Spend a few minutes looking for a bent leg. If you don't see one, you
probably have a bad chip. One program that helps identify
misbehaving chips is CheckIt, from TouchStone Software. Although
not perfect, CheckIt does a thorough memory test and is very useful
in identifying bad chips.

After you're satisfied that everything is working, put the cover back
on the computer, tighten all the screws, and then reassemble your
computer system.

Updating Your Software

The software side of the memory upgrade sometimes involves
adding a new device driver. All LIM EMS 4.0–compatible memory
expansion cards come with an expanded memory manager to control
the expanded memory. Use the setup software provided with the
card to install the expanded memory manager and configure the expanded memory.

Any applications that can use the new memory probably will—automatically. Some applications might need to be informed of the

new memory. If you're already using third-party memory managers, be sure to reinstall them or reconfigure them to work with the new memory.

If you're not using third-party memory-management software, device drivers and new commands give you access to this new memory. The next chapter describes installing the device drivers and using the new commands.

SUMMARY

Before you can take full advantage of your computer's potential, you must have plenty of memory. To add memory, you install RAM chips in your computer.

■ RAM chips are measured by their capacity and speed. The capacity is the number of bits the chip holds, typically 256 Kb or 1 Mb. The speed is measured in nanoseconds (ns): The lower the number, the faster the chip.

■ Your hardware dictates the type of RAM chip you purchase. A 1-MB RAM upgrade requires a certain type and number of chips at a certain capacity and speed.

■ You can add memory to a computer on the motherboard (if there is available room), on a LIM EMS 4.0–compatible memory expansion card, or on a special memory card.

■ A good upgrade strategy to use with 8088/8086-based and 80286-based systems is to buy a LIM EMS 4.0–compatible memory expansion card. Then backfill as much conventional memory as possible with memory on the expansion card, and configure any unused memory on the card as expanded memory.

■ With '386-based systems, you should always upgrade memory by means of the motherboard or the special memory card that fits into a 32-bit memory slot. All such memory will be extended memory.

■ Install chips with patience and care. Orient DIPs properly, and plug them in one at a time. (Be sure not to touch the legs—use a wooden object for this.)

■ After installing new memory chips, tell your computer about the new memory; flip the necessary motherboard switches, and run the Setup program on 80286-based or '386-based systems. Then reinstall or reconfigure any third-party memory-management software.

Chapter 5

Optimizing Memory with DOS 5

Having lots of memory in your PC and not being able to use it is like being 11 years old and "grounded" on a sunny day. This chapter describes how DOS 5 can help you get the most from your PC and your PC's memory. Special memory commands are covered here step by step, in the same order in which they benefit your system. You can stop making improvements at any point or continue as your hardware allows.

Note: If you're working on an 8088/8086-based PC, the information in this chapter doesn't pertain to you. See Chapters 9 and 10 for comparable information regarding your system.

THE STARTUP DISK STRATEGY

In this chapter, you'll be implementing DOS 5's memory-management commands—one at a time—by modifying the CONFIG.SYS and AUTOEXEC.BAT files. You won't, however, modify the original files. Instead, you will copy the originals to a special startup disk. You'll boot with that disk to test new memory commands and configurations, keeping your original CONFIG.SYS and AUTO-EXEC.BAT files safe and sound on the hard disk should anything go wrong.

Creating the Startup Disk

To create the Startup Disk, follow these steps:

1. Create a system disk. Put a new, blank disk in drive A, and type the following command:

   ```
   format a: /s
   ```

61

After the disk has been formatted and you see the message *System Files Transferred*, remove the disk and label it "Startup Disk." Place the disk back in drive A.

2. Copy your CONFIG.SYS and AUTOEXEC.BAT files from your hard disk to the Startup Disk. With the Startup Disk in drive A, type the commands COPY C:\CONFIG.SYS A: and COPY C:\AUTOEXEC.BAT A:

3. Edit the CONFIG.SYS and AUTOEXEC.BAT files on the Startup Disk. Be sure all the commands and device-driver locations in CONFIG.SYS and AUTOEXEC.BAT use full paths, complete with the drive letter. (And be sure the search path listed in the Path command also uses drive letters and full paths.) Use the DOS 5 Edit program to make the changes. Be sure to save the files when you've finished editing.

4. Test the Startup Disk. Press Ctrl-Alt-Del to be sure your PC boots properly from the Startup Disk. If it does, you're ready to start experimenting with DOS 5's memory commands.

If you have problems booting from the Startup Disk, carefully examine any messages. There are two general types of error messages you might see: *Bad or missing XXXX* (where XXXX is the name of a device driver) and *Bad command or filename*.

The first error message means that you forgot to add the complete path of a device driver in the CONFIG.SYS file on the Startup Disk. For example, you might see *Bad or missing \DOS\ANSI.SYS*. In this case, you forgot to add the drive letter to the path for ANSI.SYS. Use the DOS 5 Edit program to make corrections, and then save AUTOEXEC.BAT.

The second error message means that you forgot to add the complete path of a command in the AUTOEXEC.BAT file on the Startup Disk. If echo is on when AUTOEXEC.BAT executes, you'll see the command that causes the error message. To correct the problem, use the DOS 5 Edit program to insert the proper path in the AUTOEXEC.BAT file on the Startup Disk, save AUTOEXEC.BAT, and then reboot your computer.

If echo is off (if there's an @ECHO OFF command in AUTO-EXEC.BAT; echo is on by default), you won't see the command that caused the error message. Use the DOS 5 Edit program to examine the AUTOEXEC.BAT file on the Startup Disk. If you can't figure out which command caused the error message, remove the @ECHO OFF command, save AUTOEXEC.BAT, and then reboot your computer. You'll get the same error message, but this time you'll see which command is causing the error message. Then use the DOS 5 Edit program to insert the proper path in the AUTOEXEC.BAT file on the Startup Disk and save the changes.

If the DOS prompt doesn't appear for several minutes, remove the Startup Disk and reboot your PC from your hard disk. Use the Sys command to try to transfer the system files to the Startup Disk. (Put the Startup Disk in drive A and type *SYS A:*) Verify that COM-MAND.COM is on the Startup Disk. Then go back and edit CON-FIG.SYS or AUTOEXEC.BAT on the Startup Disk to see what went wrong. If none of this works, go back to step 1 with a new disk.

ACCESSING THE HMA

Most 80286-based and '386-based PCs come with 1 MB of memory. That's ordinarily configured as 640 KB of conventional memory and 384 KB of extended memory. To use upper memory blocks on a '386-based PC under DOS 5, you need at least 350 KB of extended memory. Therefore, most 1-MB '386-based PCs can create the UMBs.

To seize control of extended memory, DOS requires an extended memory manager. DOS provides an extended memory manager device driver called HIMEM.SYS, which should be familiar to Windows users. HIMEM.SYS does the following:

- Makes extended memory available to programs that use extended memory according to the XMS (Extended Memory Specification)

- Prevents system errors that can result when programs make conflicting memory requests

■ Lets 80286 and '386 microprocessors access the HMA

After HIMEM.SYS has been installed, XMS-compatible programs can use extended memory. Programs access extended memory using functions provided by the HIMEM.SYS device driver. Additionally, HIMEM.SYS gives DOS access to the HMA.

Chances are that the DOS 5 Setup program has already installed the HIMEM.SYS device driver in your CONFIG.SYS file. If not, add the following line to the CONFIG.SYS file on the Startup Disk:

```
device=c:\dos\himem.sys
```

Note: The command summary at the end of this book describes the options available with the HIMEM.SYS device driver.

Be sure to substitute the proper path if HIMEM.SYS is not in the C:\DOS subdirectory as shown. Position this command on the first line of CONFIG.SYS unless you're using a device driver that allows DOS to access hard-disk partitions larger than 32 MB. (One such device driver is DMDRVR.BIN, from OnTrak software.) The command that loads such a device driver must always be on the first line of CONFIG.SYS. If you're using a device driver such as this, position the device=c:\dos\himem.sys command on the second line of CONFIG.SYS.

Which HIMEM.SYS Should You Use?

If you have Windows, you might notice some duplication of filenames on your system. For example, both DOS 5 and Windows have files called HIMEM.SYS, RAMDRIVE.SYS, and SMARTDRV.SYS. But which do you use?

Always use the newest device drivers. Use the Dir command to check file dates, and use the file with the newest date.

The reason? The newer device drivers often fix bugs found in the older device drivers.

As an example, the following is a sample CONFIG.SYS file with HIMEM.SYS added:

```
device=c:\dos\himem.sys
files=10
shell=c:\dos\command.com c:\dos\ /p
stacks=0,0
```

When you've finished, save CONFIG.SYS and return to DOS. Reboot your PC by pressing Ctrl-Alt-Del to test the Startup Disk. (Any time you change CONFIG.SYS, you must reboot your computer for the changes to take effect.) You'll see the HIMEM.SYS startup message after the computer boots:

```
HIMEM: DOS XMS Driver, Version 2.77 - 02/27/91
XMS Specification Version 2.0
Copyright 1988-1991 Microsoft Corp.

Installed A20 handler number 1.
64K High Memory Area is available.
```

The *A20 handler* is what gives DOS access to the HMA. (If you're curious, the HMA is accessed by enabling address line 20 on 80286 and '386 microprocessors.) The message *64K High Memory Area is available* means that DOS now has access to the HMA.

If you see the message *Bad or missing HIMEM.SYS*, you probably specified an incorrect path for HIMEM.SYS in the CONFIG.SYS file. If you see *Error in CONFIG.SYS line xx*, you probably made a typo on line xx of CONFIG.SYS. (xx will be a number.) Reedit the CONFIG.SYS file on your Startup Disk, and reboot your computer again.

If you see any other messages, such as *An Extended Memory Manager is already installed* or *WARNING: The A20 Line was already enabled*, you probably have a third-party memory manager that's being installed before HIMEM.SYS. Remove the line in CONFIG.SYS that loads the other memory manager, or position the command that loads the other memory manager *after* the command that loads HIMEM.SYS in the CONFIG.SYS file on your Startup Disk. (Additional instructions for using third-party memory managers are provided in Chapter 9.)

Other messages might explain that you don't have an 80286 or '386 microprocessor or that the PC has no extended memory. In the case of the latter, refer to Chapter 4 for instructions on adding extended memory to your PC.

The major benefits of the HIMEM.SYS device driver aren't immediately apparent as far as memory usage is concerned. If you use the Mem command to view memory, you'll see only the standard display. (The memory sizes shown below might differ from what's shown on your screen, depending on how much memory is installed in your computer.)

```
A:\>mem

    655360 bytes total conventional memory
    655360 bytes available to MS-DOS
    591680 largest executable program size

    7340032 bytes total contiguous extended memory
    7340032 bytes available contiguous extended memory
```

All this command tells you is that there's a total of 640 KB of conventional memory and 7168 KB of extended memory, with 577 KB of memory available for applications.

THE DOS COMMAND

The Dos command serves two purposes:

- It moves part of DOS from conventional memory into the HMA.

- It prepares DOS to create upper memory blocks (UMBs) in upper memory on '386-based PCs with at least 350 KB of extended memory.

The format of the Dos command is

```
dos=[high¦low][umb¦noumb]
```

Options are shown in square brackets ([ ]). Mutually exclusive options (you can choose one or the other, but not both) are separated by the broken pipe character (¦). Multiple options must be separated with commas. When you specify *dos=high*, part of DOS loads into the HMA, which frees some 50 KB of conventional memory. When you specify *dos=low*, DOS loads into conventional memory. The default is dos=low.

When you specify *dos=umb*, DOS prepares to create upper memory blocks that can be used for storing device drivers and memory-resident programs. If you specify *dos=noumb*, the UMBs are not created. The default is dos=noumb.

Note: The umb option works only on '386-based PCs with at least 350 KB of extended memory. The HIMEM.SYS device driver must be installed before this command can be used. If you have an 8088/8086-based or 80286-based PC, the umb option is ignored by DOS.

To load part of DOS into the HMA and thereby free some 50 KB of conventional memory, put the dos=high command into the CONFIG.SYS file on the Startup Disk. The dos=high command should go on the line following *device=c:\DOS\HIMEM.SYS*.

For example, the CONFIG.SYS file presented earlier in this chapter should look like this:

```
device=c:\dos\himem.sys
dos=high
files=10
shell=c:\dos\command.com c:\dos\  /p
stacks=0,0
```

Save CONFIG.SYS on the Startup Disk, and then reboot your PC to test the change.

After your PC boots, you'll see the HIMEM.SYS message. You might see the following error:

```
HMA not available: loading DOS low
```

This means that another memory manager has loaded itself into the HMA and DOS was unable to load there. If this happens, edit the CONFIG.SYS file on the Startup Disk. Make HIMEM.SYS the first memory manager installed, followed by the dos=high command. Save CONFIG.SYS, and then reboot your computer again.

Here is where you hit pay dirt. Use the Mem command to see how
much more conventional memory you have:

```
A:\>mem

    655360 bytes total conventional memory
    655360 bytes available to MS-DOS
    640096 largest executable program size

   7340032 bytes total contiguous extended memory
         0 bytes available contiguous extended memory
   7274496 bytes available XMS memory
           MS-DOS resident in High Memory Area
```

The output of the command has changed slightly; more information
is displayed. First note the increased conventional memory: 625 KB
(640,096 bytes) is available! Next note that the HMA's memory (64
KB) has been subtracted from extended memory. You're also told
that DOS is now in the HMA. Finally all remaining extended memory is available to applications that need it.

Preparing for UMBs

The second optional parameter of the Dos command is umb ! noumb.
On a '386-based PC, when you specify *dos=umb*, DOS prepares to
create upper memory blocks. By itself, dos=umb doesn't create upper memory blocks, but it sets the stage for doing so at a later time.
This will be covered a little later in this chapter.

On your Startup Disk, edit the CONFIG.SYS file. Look for the line
containing the Dos command, and edit it to read as follows:

```
dos=high,umb
```

This command places part of DOS into the HMA and tells DOS to
prepare to create UMBs.

SIMULATING EXPANDED MEMORY

You'll soon discover that the greatest memory benefits exist for the
'386-based PCs—which makes sense given the powerful memory-
mapping capabilities of the '386 microprocessor. Only on '386-
based PCs can extended memory simulate expanded memory under

DOS 5. If you have an 80286-based system, look forward to Chapter 9, but first skip to the section in this chapter titled "Updating the Hard Drive."

There's one good reason to want expanded memory on a '386-based PC: A lot of DOS applications use expanded memory. Spreadsheets, paint programs, word processors, and other DOS applications can often use a few kilobytes of expanded memory.

There are two steps to simulating expanded memory on a '386-based PC under DOS 5: The first is creating UMBs using the Dos command; the second is telling the EMM386.EXE expanded memory emulator to simulate expanded memory using extended memory.

Using EMM386.EXE

DOS 5 uses EMM386.EXE to simulate expanded memory by using extended memory on '386-based PCs. Despite its EXE filename extension, this file is a device driver and is installed in CONFIG.SYS.

The EMM386.EXE device driver has the following basic format:

```
device=c:\dos\emm386.exe [[memory[ram]]:noems]
```

Note that many more options are available for EMM386.EXE. For now, only the basic options necessary for creating UMBs and using extended memory to simulate expanded memory are covered. For a complete list of EMM386.EXE options, see the Command Reference at the end of this book, or check your DOS 5 manual.

There are two basic options: *ram* and *noems*. If you specify both options, noems takes precedence. The noems option tells DOS to create UMBs using extended memory without simulating any expanded memory. Use the noems option when you want UMBs and access to all your extended memory.

The ram option creates UMBs and also simulates expanded memory. By default, EMM386.EXE simulates 256 KB of expanded memory. If you need more, specify the amount you need (in kilobytes) with the *memory* option. You can also make use of the

memory option without the ram option—this simulates expanded
memory without creating UMBs.

The memory option is a number ranging from 16 (for 16 KB) to
32,768 (for 32 MB). You can simulate as much expanded memory as
the amount of available extended memory in your computer. Remember, the HMA takes 64 KB of extended memory, creating UMBs
takes some extended memory, you might have a RAM disk loaded
into extended memory, and so on.

Adding EMM386.EXE to CONFIG.SYS

Edit the CONFIG.SYS file on the Startup Disk. To simulate expanded memory or to create UMBs, you must load the EMM386.EXE
device driver *after* loading HIMEM.SYS. A good position would be
immediately following the dos=high,umb command. Insert the following line:

```
device=c:\dos\emm386.exe
```

Be sure to specify the proper path; in this example, C:\DOS is
assumed. Also, you should note that the name is EMM386.*EXE—not*
EMM386.SYS.

To properly configure EMM386.EXE, you need to think about your
software and answer the following questions:

1. Do any of your applications need expanded memory? If the
   answer is no, such as when you're running Windows, skip to
   step 3. If yes, then figure out how much you need. If you have a
   '386-based computer with 2 MB of memory, 512 KB is a good
   value. (If you're uncertain as to the amount you need, don't
   specify anything: As a default, EMM386.EXE will simulate
   only 256 KB, which should be OK on all '386-based computers
   with 1 MB of memory.) Specify *512*, or the value you've settled
   on, after the EMM386.EXE command in the CONFIG.SYS file
   on the Startup Disk:

   ```
   device=c:\dos\emm386.exe 512
   ```

2. Does your hardware or software require any specific EMM386.EXE options? If so, look the options up in the Command Reference at the end of this book, and add options as required. You might also want to check your hardware manual with regard to the ''page frame'' location.

3. Will you be using UMBs? If yes, add the ram option as the last item on the line. However, if you're using Windows or if you've decided not to simulate any expanded memory, specify the noems option. For example, to create UMBs on a '386-based PC and leave the maximum amount of extended memory for running Windows, add the following line to the CONFIG.SYS file on the Startup Disk:

```
device=c:\dos\emm386.exe noems
```

If you want to create the UMBs and simulate 512 KB of expanded memory, the line should look like this:

```
device=c:\dos\emm386.exe 512 ram
```

You can specify *device=c:\dos\emm386.exe ram* if you want only 256 KB of expanded memory plus UMBs.

With the addition of the EMM386.EXE device driver, the sample CONFIG.SYS file would look something like this:

```
device=c:\dos\himem.sys
dos=high,umb
device=c:\dos\emm386.exe 512 ram
files=10
shell=c:\dos\command.com c:\dos\ /p
stacks=0,0
```

Finish editing the CONFIG.SYS file, and save it on the Startup Disk. Reboot your computer.

After booting and after HIMEM.SYS's message appears, you'll see the display from the EMM386.EXE device driver on your screen.

```
MICROSOFT Expanded Memory Manager 386  Version 4.20.06X
(C) Copyright Microsoft Corporation 1986, 1990

EMM386 successfully installed.

    Available expanded memory . . . . . . .    512 KB

    LIM/EMS version . . . . . . . . . . . . .   4.0
    Total expanded memory pages . . . . . . .    56
    Available expanded memory pages . . . . .    32
    Total handles . . . . . . . . . . . . . .    64
    Active handles  . . . . . . . . . . . . .     1
    Page frame segment  . . . . . . . . . . . E000 H

    Total upper memory available  . . . . . .    59 KB
    Largest Upper Memory Block available  . .    35 KB
    Upper memory starting address . . . . . . C800 H

EMM386 Active.
```

The display confirms the amount of expanded memory you have
available (in this example, 512 KB). The next list of items describes
the expanded memory manager device driver information. (This information is very technical; you don't need to know what it means.)
Finally, information about the UMBs is displayed. In this example,
59 KB of memory is available for storage in the UMBs.

If you've specified the noems option, the display from the
EMM386.EXE device driver might look something like this:

```
MICROSOFT Expanded Memory Manager 386  Version 4.20.06X
(C) Copyright Microsoft Corporation 1986, 1990

EMM386 successfully installed.

    Expanded memory services unavailable.

    Total upper memory available  . . . . . .    63 KB
    Largest Upper Memory Block available  . .    63 KB
    Upper memory starting address . . . . . . C800 H

EMM386 Active.
```

Expanded memory services unavailable means that no extended
memory is simulating expanded memory. However, approximately
63 KB of upper memory is available above for storing device drivers
and memory-resident software. (More upper memory is available
when no extended memory is simulating expanded memory. This is
because no EMS page frame is required. Some PCs can gain access to
extra upper memory even while simulating expanded memory; this
is covered in Chapter 6.)

Simply creating the UMBs doesn't automatically increase available conventional memory; you must move a device driver or memory-resident program to a UMB before you notice the difference. However, the Mem command will alert you to the presence of the new memory:

```
655360 bytes total conventional memory
655360 bytes available to MS-DOS
631664 largest executable program size

7340032 bytes total contiguous extended memory
      0 bytes available contiguous extended memory
7121920 bytes available XMS memory
        MS-DOS resident in High Memory Area
```

A more detailed view of what's going on can be seen by issuing the Mem command with the /classify switch (Figure 5-1). When you

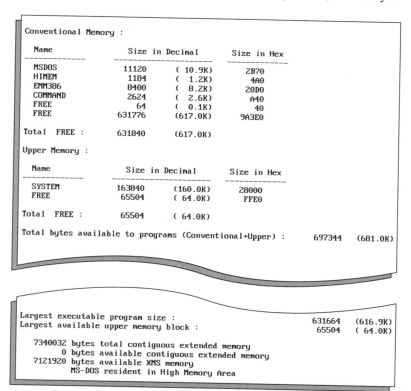

```
Conventional Memory :

    Name              Size in Decimal        Size in Hex
-------------       --------------------    --------------
    MSDOS              11120    ( 10.9K)        2B70
    HIMEM               1184    (  1.2K)         4A0
    EMM386              8400    (  8.2K)        20D0
    COMMAND             2624    (  2.6K)         A40
    FREE                  64    (  0.1K)          40
    FREE              631776    (617.0K)        9A3E0

Total  FREE :         631840    (617.0K)

Upper Memory :

    Name              Size in Decimal        Size in Hex
-------------       --------------------    --------------
    SYSTEM            163840    (160.0K)        28000
    FREE               65504    ( 64.0K)         FFE0

Total  FREE :          65504    ( 64.0K)

Total bytes available to programs (Conventional+Upper) :    697344    (681.0K)
```

```
Largest executable program size :              631664    (616.9K)
Largest available upper memory block :          65504    ( 64.0K)

   7340032 bytes total contiguous extended memory
         0 bytes available contiguous extended memory
   7121920 bytes available XMS memory
           MS-DOS resident in High Memory Area
```

Figure 5-1. *The output of* mem /classify *when UMBs are active.*

look at conventional memory, you can see the HIMEM and EMM386 device drivers. A new section—*Upper Memory*—appears, describing what's going on in upper memory. The *Total bytes available to programs* value now includes both conventional and upper memory.

Running EMM386 from the Command Line

EMM386.EXE can also be run as a stand-alone program if EMM386.EXE has been installed as a device driver. From the command line, it provides the current status of expanded memory support or allows you to turn expanded memory support on or off. It also enables or disables support for a Weitek math coprocessor (a special chip you can install in some computers that handles mathematical operations). The command-line format is

```
emm386 [on:off:auto] [w=on:w=off]
```

The first option is either *on*, *off*, or *auto*. On turns expanded memory support on, off turns expanded memory support off, and auto activates auto sense mode, in which expanded memory support is enabled only when a program requests expanded memory. The default is on. Note that EMM386.EXE must already be installed as a device driver; otherwise, this command has no effect. Also note that expanded memory support can't be disabled if UMBs have been created or if any applications are using expanded memory.

The second option is either *w=on* or *w=off* and is used to activate support for the Weitek math coprocessor. The default is w=off. As before, EMM386.EXE must already be installed as a device driver for this command to have any effect.

Without any options, emm386 displays the same information you see when your computer first boots—informative stuff, but not extremely practical.

Your computer now has the following:

■ An extended memory manager (HIMEM.SYS)

■ Access to the HMA for storing part of DOS

- An expanded memory emulator (EMM386.EXE)

- Upper memory blocks

Of course, there's still potential. Part of DOS is now in the HMA, but UMBs beckon. Putting device drivers and memory-resident programs in UMBs is covered in the next chapter.

UPDATING THE HARD DRIVE

Before you copy CONFIG.SYS from the Startup Disk back to your hard disk, make copies of the CONFIG.SYS and AUTOEXEC.BAT files on your hard disk. Type the following commands:

```
copy c:\config.sys c:\config.old
copy c:\autoexec.bat c:\autoexec.old
```

That way, you'll have copies of these files if you ever have problems with your new CONFIG.SYS and AUTOEXEC.BAT files.

If you're satisfied with the Startup Disk's CONFIG.SYS file, put the Startup Disk in drive A, and copy the CONFIG.SYS file from the Startup Disk back to the root directory in drive C.

```
A:\>copy a:\config.sys c:\
```

Remove the Startup Disk from drive A, and reboot your computer. You're now one step closer to mastering memory on your computer.

SUMMARY

To optimize your computer's memory potential under DOS 5, you start with HIMEM.SYS and the Dos command. If you have a '386-based computer, you also create UMBs and, optionally, simulate expanded memory by using extended memory.

- DOS 5's extended memory manager is a device driver called HIMEM.SYS. HIMEM.SYS also gives DOS access to the HMA on 80286-based and '386-based PCs with extended memory.

- The Dos command loads part of DOS into the HMA. This frees some 50 KB of conventional memory.

- The Dos command must come after the command that loads the HIMEM.SYS device driver.

- The Dos command also prepares DOS to create upper memory blocks (UMBs) on '386-based computers with at least 350 KB of extended memory.

- The EMM386.EXE expanded memory emulator serves two purposes: It maps extended memory into upper memory, thereby creating UMBs; and it uses extended memory to simulate expanded memory on a '386-based computer.

- If you need to simulate a specific amount of expanded memory, include that amount (in KB) at the end of the line that installs the EMM386.EXE device driver. If you also want to activate UMBs, include the ram switch as well.

- If you want access to UMBs but don't want to simulate expanded memory, such as when you're running Windows, use the noems option when installing the EMM386.EXE device driver.

- After they've been created, UMBs can be used to store device drivers and memory-resident programs.

Chapter 6

Loading High

In the last chapter, you prepared your computer to work more efficiently by moving part of DOS into the high memory area and by creating the upper memory blocks. In this chapter, you'll take full advantage of this extra memory by using two DOS commands to free conventional memory: Devicehigh, which moves device drivers into UMBs; and Loadhigh, which moves memory-resident programs into UMBs.

Note: Because these device drivers and memory-resident programs are moved into upper memory blocks (UMBs), and because UMBs can be created only on '386-based PCs with at least 350 KB of extended memory, the techniques in this chapter will not work on 8088/8086-based or 80286-based PCs. Refer to Chapter 9 for solutions specific to those machines.

WHY LOAD HIGH?

Consider the ultimate '386-based computer: fast microprocessor, fast hard disk, and an abundance of memory. You've carefully added several megabytes of extended memory, which can simulate expanded memory as needed using EMM386.EXE. Yet no matter how much memory you have, DOS still uses only the 640 KB of conventional memory to run applications. It's that 640 KB of conventional memory that's crucial. Anything in conventional memory besides your application is a potential RAM waster.

To get more from the 640 KB of conventional memory, enterprising DOS users have developed a number of tricks. Prior to the memory-management commands introduced with DOS 5, these secrets have included doing without some memory-resident programs and neglecting to buy memory-hungry programs.

77

Managing that 640 KB of conventional memory without help is a chore. You might like to use a pop-up calculator with your spreadsheet but only be able to use one or the other at any given time. It just ain't fair.

Part of DOS can be moved to the HMA, giving you an additional 50 KB of conventional memory. But suppose you still want to install a network device driver and a mouse device driver and use a memory-resident pop-up calculator. And now that you have a little more memory, you think about using that keyboard-enhancer program that's gathering dust on the shelf. The basic problem is still there: You have to load those device drivers and programs into conventional memory, which cuts back on the 640 KB of conventional memory. Or do you?

Loading high is the process of moving device drivers and memory-resident programs out of conventional memory and into UMBs. This lets you use those programs *and* keep most of the 640 KB of conventional memory for your memory-hungry applications—the best of both worlds.

Moving Programs

DOS 5 can transfer just about any device driver or memory-resident program into an upper memory block. To find out which potentially movable device drivers and memory-resident programs are loaded and the amount of free memory in the UMBs, use the following command:

```
mem /c ¦ more
```

Figure 6-1 illustrates the typical result.

In Figure 6-1 and on your own screen, locate MSDOS, HIMEM, and EMM386 in the Conventional Memory section of the listing. Although those programs are anchored in memory, any device driver or memory-resident program listed after them other than COMMAND is movable. In Figure 6-1, that includes the ANSI.SYS and MOUSE.SYS device drivers and the DOSKEY memory-resident program.

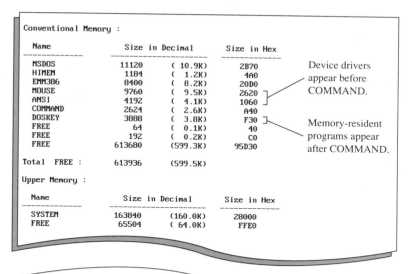

```
Conventional Memory :

    Name                   Size in Decimal        Size in Hex
-------------           ------------------      --------------
    MSDOS                  11120    ( 10.9K)         2B70        Device drivers
    HIMEM                   1184    (  1.2K)          4A0         appear before
    EMM386                  8400    (  8.2K)         20D0         COMMAND.
    MOUSE                   9760    (  9.5K)         2620  ⌉
    ANSI                    4192    (  4.1K)         1060  ⌋
    COMMAND                 2624    (  2.6K)          A40
    DOSKEY                  3888    (  3.8K)          F30  ⌉      Memory-resident
    FREE                      64    (  0.1K)           40         programs appear
    FREE                     192    (  0.2K)           C0         after COMMAND.
    FREE                  613680    (599.3K)        95D30

Total  FREE :             613936    (599.5K)

Upper Memory :

    Name                   Size in Decimal        Size in Hex
-------------           ------------------      --------------
    SYSTEM                163840    (160.0K)        28000
    FREE                   65504    ( 64.0K)         FFE0
```

```
Total  FREE :             65504    ( 64.0K)

Total bytes available to programs (Conventional+Upper) :        679440    (663.5K)
Largest executable program size :                               613680    (599.3K)
Largest available upper memory block :                           65504    ( 64.0K)

    7340032 bytes total contiguous extended memory
          0 bytes available contiguous extended memory
    7121920 bytes available XMS memory
            MS-DOS resident in High Memory Area
```

Figure 6-1. *MOUSE, ANSI, and DOSKEY wait to be loaded high.*

By examining the information, you can determine if the device drivers and memory-resident program will fit into a UMB: In this example, ANSI.SYS uses only 4.1 KB; MOUSE.SYS uses 9.6 KB; and DOSKEY uses 3.8 KB—17.5 KB in all. The largest available upper memory block is 64 KB. Therefore, these device drivers and the memory-resident program can be "loaded high"—with room to spare.

All you need are the commands necessary to load device drivers and memory-resident programs into UMBs. For device drivers, you need the Devicehigh command. For memory-resident programs, you need the Loadhigh command.

Note: As in previous chapters, you'll be making changes to your Startup Disk before you actually change files on the hard disk.

THE DEVICEHIGH COMMAND

The Devicehigh command loads device drivers into an upper memory block. Devicehigh works in the same way as the Device command. In fact, for most device drivers all you need to do is change each Device command to a Devicehigh command—almost a search and replace. The syntax of the Devicehigh command is

```
Devicehigh=Driver
```

where *Driver* is the path and name of a device driver. This is where the Startup Disk comes in really handy. Loading some device drivers into UMBs can be tricky, which is why changes made to CONFIG.SYS will be made first on the Startup Disk and then transferred back to your hard disk when you're sure everything works.

Your strategy will be to load one device driver at a time into a UMB, changing the appropriate Device command to Devicehigh. For practice, the first device driver to load into a UMB will be the ANSI.SYS device driver.

Loading ANSI.SYS into a UMB

1. **Use the DOS 5 Edit program to edit the CONFIG.SYS file on the Startup Disk.** Insert the following Devicehigh command to load the ANSI.SYS device driver into a UMB (or edit the existing Device command for ANSI.SYS):

   ```
   devicehigh=c:\dos\ansi.sys
   ```

   Remember to specify the proper path for ANSI.SYS. (In this example, the C:\DOS subdirectory is assumed.)

   Note how smooth the change was. On most computers, you only need to change *device* to *devicehigh*.

2. **Save the CONFIG.SYS file and exit to DOS.** Reboot the computer. The computer will boot as it did the last time you booted with the Startup Disk; ANSI.SYS offers no visual feedback when it loads.

3. **Type the command** *mem /c ¦ more* **and locate** ANSI.SYS.
ANSI will be in the Upper Memory section of the listing,
loaded into a UMB. You've just released 4.1 KB of conventional memory. (Of course, if you merely added ANSI.SYS for
this test, you haven't released any conventional memory; but
the test is an important learning step.)

Loading Device Drivers High

On your Startup Disk, locate another device driver, and change the
Device command to Devicehigh. For example, to move a Microsoft
mouse device driver into a UMB (and thereby save 14 KB of conventional memory), edit

```
device=c:\mouse\mouse.sys /c1
```

to read

```
devicehigh=c:\mouse\mouse.sys /c1
```

Note how the /c1 switch (which tells the mouse device driver to use
serial port 1—COM1) is retained after the device driver's name.
Start changing the Device commands in the CONFIG.SYS file on
your Startup Disk to Devicehigh—but only one Device command at
a time. Save each change to CONFIG.SYS, exit to DOS, and reboot
your computer.

Check the results with the *mem /c ¦ more* command after booting.
After moving the MOUSE.SYS and ANSI.SYS device drivers, the
Mem /c command produces the display shown in Figure 6-2.

Check out those numbers! 613.0 KB of free conventional memory is
good—and getting better!

Continue experimenting on your own. But note that in some in-
stances, a device driver might not move into a UMB. Don't panic:
The device driver loaded into conventional memory for some unknown reason.

```
Conventional Memory :

   Name                 Size in Decimal         Size in Hex
   ------------         ----------------         -----------
   MSDOS                11120      ( 10.9K)       2B70
   HIMEM                 1184      (  1.2K)       4A0
   EMM386                8400      (  8.2K)       20D0
   COMMAND               2624      (  2.6K)       A40
   DOSKEY                3888      (  3.8K)       F30
   FREE                    64      (  0.1K)       40
   FREE                   192      (  0.2K)       C0
   FREE                627664      (613.0K)       993D0

Total  FREE :           627920      (613.2K)

Upper Memory :

   Name                 Size in Decimal         Size in Hex
   ------------         ----------------         -----------
   SYSTEM               163840      (160.0K)       28000
   MOUSE                  9760      (  9.5K)       2620
   ANSI                   4192      (  4.1K)       1060
   FREE                  51504      ( 50.3K)       C930
```

```
Total  FREE :           51504      ( 50.3K)

Total bytes available to programs (Conventional+Upper) :     679424   (663.5K)
Largest executable program size :                            627664   (613.0K)
Largest available upper memory block :                        51504   ( 50.3K)

    7340032 bytes total contiguous extended memory
          0 bytes available contiguous extended memory
    7121920 bytes available XMS memory
            MS-DOS resident in High Memory Area
```

Figure 6-2. *MOUSE and ANSI are now in upper memory blocks.*

Beware Expanding Device Drivers

The Devicehigh command is smart enough to figure out when a device driver or memory-resident program will not fit into a UMB. If the device driver or memory-resident program won't fit into a UMB, Devicehigh loads the device driver (or memory-resident program) into conventional memory instead. However, some device drivers need extra memory after they're loaded. If the UMB the device driver is loaded into doesn't have enough memory for the device driver, your computer might lock up.

You can solve this problem by specifying the minimum amount of memory the device driver needs before it can be loaded into a UMB.

Use Devicehigh's size option. The format is

```
devicehigh size=xxx driver
```

where *xxx* is the minimum number of bytes, in hexadecimal, that the device driver needs before it can be loaded into a UMB. The size option tells the Devicehigh command how much space the driver will occupy. (Use the Mem /c command to determine the device driver's size. Be sure to find and use the device driver's size in hex, not decimal.) If the UMB doesn't have this much free memory, the Devicehigh command loads the device driver into conventional memory instead.

driver is the path and name of the device driver, followed by whatever options the device driver requires.

For example, consider the fictional RAMPIG.SYS device driver. RAMPIG.SYS needs an extra 2 KB of RAM after loading. To find RAMPIG's minimum memory requirements, use the *mem /c ¦ more* command. Locate RAMPIG in the Conventional Memory section of the output from the Mem command. It might appear as follows:

```
RAMPIG          4082    ( 4.0K)        FF2
```

That value, 4 KB or FF2 hex, is the true amount of memory RAMPIG.SYS needs. To load RAMPIG into an upper memory block, you would use the following Devicehigh command in your CONFIG.SYS file:

```
devicehigh size=ff2 c:\bloat\rampig.sys /oink
```

You would use the *mem /c ¦ more* command to confirm that the driver had moved.

If your computer locks up after a device driver has been moved to a UMB, boot from your hard disk, and check that device driver's size with Mem /c. Then edit CONFIG.SYS on the Startup Disk to load the device driver into a UMB, and include the size parameter. But note that even with the size parameter, some device drivers simply won't work correctly when loaded into an upper memory block.

Although DOS 5 can load a device driver or a memory-resident program anywhere in conventional or upper memory, you might encounter a device driver that flat-out refuses to work correctly in an upper memory block. This is the reason for using the Startup Disk: It's best to test loading a device driver into a UMB from a Startup Disk first to see if it works correctly. If you have problems loading a device driver into a UMB, load the device driver into conventional memory instead.

UMB-Approved DOS Device Drivers

DOS 5 comes with 11 device drivers. Of those, you can load the following into upper memory blocks:

DISPLAY.SYS	PRINTER.SYS
DRIVER.SYS	RAMDRIVE.SYS
EGA.SYS	SETVER.EXE
ANSI.SYS	SMARTDRV.SYS

Of course, you probably don't want all of these device drivers loaded at once.

Note that RAMDRIVE.SYS and SMARTDRV.SYS can be loaded into UMBs. Even though you may specify a 2-MB RAM disk or a 512-KB disk cache—way too big for a UMB—these device drivers can be loaded into UMBs. The secret is that, although the device drivers will be in UMBs, the actual RAM disk or disk cache will be created in conventional, extended, or expanded memory (whichever you specify). So don't be afraid to put these device drivers in UMBs, but don't forget to first perform a test on the Startup Disk.

Keep On Going!

Continue converting your device drivers to load into UMBs one at a time. Do this until you've totally optimized memory, loading as many device drivers as possible into upper memory blocks.

After you're satisfied that as many device drivers as possible are loading into UMBs, copy the CONFIG.SYS file from the Startup Disk back to your hard disk: Put the Startup Disk in drive A, and type the following command:

```
copy a:config.sys c:\
```

THE LOADHIGH COMMAND

The Loadhigh command loads memory-resident programs into upper memory blocks. Although Loadhigh works in the same way as the Devicehigh command, Loadhigh is a bit easier to use. Here is the format:

```
loadhigh filename
```

filename is the path and name of a memory-resident program that you want to load into a UMB. It must be a memory-resident program. The filename is followed by any switches or parameters that would normally follow it on the command line.

Loadhigh is incredibly simple to use: You place *loadhigh* in front of any memory-resident program you want to load into a UMB, either

Devicehigh Tips

- Use the Startup Disk to test loading device drivers into UMBs first. If your computer locks up, you can reboot your computer from the hard disk.

- If loading a device driver into a UMB causes your computer to lock up, experiment with Devicehigh's size option for that device driver. If your computer still locks up, try changing the order in which device drivers are loaded. If that doesn't work, then just don't load that particular device driver into a UMB!

- Load larger device drivers first. Devicehigh is smart and will sandwich smaller device drivers into smaller UMBs when it can. But if you save your largest device drivers to be loaded last, they might not fit.

at the DOS prompt or (more likely) in your AUTOEXEC.BAT file. To make life even easier, you can abbreviate Loadhigh as *LH*.

The strategy for loading memory-resident programs into UMBs is identical to the strategy for moving device drivers: Load the memory-resident programs one at a time, placing the Loadhigh command before the memory-resident program's name in AUTOEXEC.BAT. Then reboot your computer, and use the Mem /c command to confirm that the memory-resident program is in a UMB. Be sure the memory-resident program still works. For practice, the first memory-resident program to load into a UMB will be the Doskey keyboard–command line enhancement program.

Loading Doskey into a UMB

The Doskey program is a handy keyboard–command line enhancement program that comes with DOS 5. In my opinion, every PC using DOS 5 should have it installed. (A complete guide to Doskey is provided in Van Wolverton's *Supercharging MS-DOS,* also from Microsoft Press.)

The following line, which is part of your AUTOEXEC.BAT file, installs Doskey in conventional memory:

```
c:\dos\doskey
```

(Remember to substitute the correct path for Doskey. In this example, the C:\DOS subdirectory is assumed.)

To load Doskey into a UMB instead of conventional memory, add the Loadhigh command to the previous example in the AUTO-EXEC.BAT file on the Startup Disk:

```
loadhigh c:\dos\doskey
```

Save the AUTOEXEC.BAT file, exit to DOS, and then reboot your computer.

After your computer boots, you'll see the message *DOSKey installed,* which tells you DOS has loaded Doskey. Confirm Doskey's location in memory by typing the *mem /c ¦ more* command. Doskey should now be in an upper memory block.

In Figure 6-3, you can see that conventional memory is now completely devoid of device drivers and memory-resident programs; DOSKEY is now in a UMB, along with the MOUSE.SYS and ANSI.SYS device drivers. All device drivers and memory-resident programs work, but they're located in UMBs rather than conventional memory. Comparing Figure 6-3 to Figure 6-1, you can see there are 17,904 more bytes of conventional memory, for a total of 631,840 bytes of conventional memory available to applications.

On your own computer, check to see that Doskey is in an upper memory block. If you're using any other memory-resident programs, such as third-party keyboard enhancers, print spoolers, RAM disks—even the venerable SideKick—experiment with loading

```
Conventional Memory :

    Name                Size in Decimal       Size in Hex
 --------------       --------------------    --------------
    MSDOS                 11120    ( 10.9K)       2B70
    HIMEM                  1184    (  1.2K)        4A0
    EMM386                 8400    (  8.2K)       20D0
    COMMAND                2624    (  2.6K)        A40
    FREE                     64    (  0.1K)         40
    FREE                 631776    (617.0K)       9A3E0

 Total  FREE :          631840    (617.0K)

Upper Memory :

    Name                Size in Decimal       Size in Hex
 --------------       --------------------    --------------
    SYSTEM               163840    (160.0K)      28000
    MOUSE                  9760    (  9.5K)       2620
    ANSI                   4192    (  4.1K)       1060
    DOSKEY                 3888    (  3.8K)        F30
    FREE                    192    (  0.2K)         C0
    FREE                  47392    ( 46.3K)       B920
```

```
Total  FREE :           47584    ( 46.5K)

Total bytes available to programs (Conventional+Upper) :    679424    (663.5K)
Largest executable program size :                           631776    (617.0K)
Largest available upper memory block :                       47392    ( 46.3K)

    7340032 bytes total contiguous extended memory
          0 bytes available contiguous extended memory
    7121920 bytes available XMS memory
          MS-DOS resident in High Memory Area
```

Figure 6-3. *DOSKEY is now in an upper memory block.*

them into UMBs as well. Remember to load memory-resident programs into UMBs one at a time, using the Startup Disk for testing. Tips and suggestions are provided in the section titled "Loadhigh Tips."

Note: Although you can specify Doskey more than once in your AUTOEXEC.BAT file (for example, to create macros), you should use Loadhigh only with the initial Doskey command.

Loadhigh Tips

- When Loadhigh can't load a memory-resident program into a UMB, it will instead load it into conventional memory. If this happens, experiment with changing the order in which you load memory-resident programs into UMBs before giving up.

- If your system locks up intermittently after loading a memory-resident program into a UMB, disable loading the program by putting a REM command in front of the Loadhigh command that loads the program, and reboot your computer. If the computer stops locking up, edit AUTOEXEC.BAT to load the memory-resident program into conventional memory, save AUTOEXEC.BAT, and then reboot your computer.

UMB-Approved DOS 5 Memory-Resident Programs

The first real memory-resident program was DOS's own Print program, which first appeared with DOS version 2.0. Since that time, DOS has played host to several memory-resident programs. Those that follow can be used with the Loadhigh command:

APPEND.EXE	GRAPHICS.COM	NLSFUNC.EXE
DOSKEY.COM	KEYB.COM	PRINT.EXE
DOSSHELL.COM	MODE.COM	SHARE.EXE

DOS programs not on this list should not be used with Loadhigh.

The list of commercially available memory-resident programs seems endless. Nearly all of them (those that can fit, at least) can be moved into a UMB, thereby freeing conventional memory. Keep in mind that Loadhigh isn't a miracle worker: If a memory-resident program is too big to fit into a UMB, Loadhigh will simply load it into conventional memory. Do not use Loadhigh with non-memory-resident programs: The results will be unpredictable.

As with device drivers, the best way to find out which memory-resident programs will work properly when loaded into UMBs is to experiment. Use your Startup Disk until you're certain that every memory-resident program loaded into a UMB is working properly. Then copy the AUTOEXEC.BAT file from the Startup Disk to your hard disk.

GROWING EXTRA UMBS

Welcome to a DOS 5 configuration in which you can load all your device drivers and memory-resident programs into UMBs...up until there's no unused memory in UMBs. The Mem /c command shown in Figure 6-4 has only 9.4 KB of memory free in UMBs. That's not enough for another device driver or memory-resident program. But there's a way to let some computers create another 64-KB UMB.

Some computers can get another 64-KB UMB when you're using the EMM386.EXE expanded memory emulator to simulate expanded memory. That's even more memory for your device drivers and memory-resident programs. (Unfortunately, this trick won't work when you're using the noems option.)

The EMM386.EXE expanded memory emulator has a slew of options that let you customize how it behaves. If you don't specify any options, EMM386.EXE makes some assumptions about your computer. One of those assumptions deals with the location of the page frame, the 64-KB area in upper memory where pages of expanded memory are mapped.

```
Conventional Memory :

   Name               Size in Decimal        Size in Hex
 --------------      -------------------     -------------
   MSDOS                 11120   ( 10.9K)        2B70
   HIMEM                  1184   (  1.2K)         4A0
   EMM386                 8400   (  8.2K)        20D0
   COMMAND                2624   (  2.6K)         A40
   FREE                     64   (  0.1K)          40
   FREE                 631776   (617.0K)        9A3E0

 Total  FREE :          631840   (617.0K)

 Upper Memory :

   Name               Size in Decimal        Size in Hex
 --------------      -------------------     -------------
   SYSTEM               163840   (160.0K)       28000
   MOUSE                  9760   (  9.5K)        2620
   ANSI                   4192   (  4.1K)        1060
   DOSKEY                 3888   (  3.8K)         F30
   FREE                    192   (  0.2K)          C0
   FREE                   9467   (  9.2K)        2400
```

```
 Total  FREE :            9659   (  9.4K)

 Total bytes available to programs (Conventional+Upper) :   641499   (626.4K)
 Largest executable program size :                          631776   (617.0K)
 Largest available upper memory block :                       9467   (  9.2K)

    7340032 bytes total contiguous extended memory
          0 bytes available contiguous extended memory
    7121920 bytes available XMS memory
            MS-DOS resident in High Memory Area
```

Figure 6-4. *A system with limited upper memory.*

When you run EMM386 from the DOS prompt, EMM386 displays something like Figure 6-5.

Type *emm386* at the DOS prompt, and examine the output. Look for the line that reads *Page frame segment.* That's the segment of memory that EMM386 uses as the page frame. In this example, and probably on your computer as well, EMM386 uses segment D000 H. (The H stands for hexadecimal.)

Why segment D000? Segments D000 and E000 are unused on many computers. On PS/2 computers, segment E000 holds special BIOS extensions. But most garden-variety IBM compatibles and clones lack these extensions.

```
MICROSOFT Expanded Memory Manager 386  Version 4.20.06X
(C) Copyright Microsoft Corporation 1986, 1990

EMM386 successfully installed.

    Available expanded memory . . . . . . . .   512 KB

    LIM/EMS version . . . . . . . . . . . . .   4.0
    Total expanded memory pages . . . . . . .   56
    Available expanded memory pages . . . . .   32
    Total handles . . . . . . . . . . . . . .   64
    Active handles  . . . . . . . . . . . . .   1
    Page frame segment  . . . . . . . . . . .   D000 H

    Total upper memory available  . . . . . .   31 KB
    Largest Upper Memory Block available  . .   31 KB
    Upper memory starting address . . . . . .   C800 H

EMM386 Active.
```

Figure 6-5. *The result of EMM386.*

If you're not using a PS/2 and are somewhat certain that your computer is not using segment E000 (generally a safe assumption), you can change EMM386's page frame from segment D000 to segment E000. (You might have to disable any shadow RAM first.) The end result is another 64-KB UMB in which to store your device drivers and memory-resident programs.

On your Startup Disk, edit the CONFIG.SYS file. Change the command that installs EMM386.EXE to read

```
device=c:\dos\emm386.exe 512 frame=e000 ram
```

Essentially, you're placing the frame=e000 option between the amount of expanded memory you want and the ram option.

Save CONFIG.SYS, exit to DOS, and reboot your computer. If you see a message saying *Option ROM or RAM detected within page frame* or *E000 page frame address not recommended* or *Unable to set page frame*, you can't change the page frame to segment E000. Remove the frame=e000 option from the command that installs the EMM386.EXE device driver, and reboot again.

If changing the location of the page frame worked (and it should on most computers), your computer will boot normally. Confirm the location of the page frame by typing *emm386* again at the DOS prompt. You'll see that the page frame is now segment E000.

Now type the *mem /c ¦ more* command. Look at the Upper Memory summary, and examine the amount of free memory. The computer depicted in Figure 6-6 now has 95 KB free! That's an improvement of 64 KB.

```
MICROSOFT Expanded Memory Manager 386  Version 4.20.06X
(C) Copyright Microsoft Corporation 1986, 1990

EMM386 successfully installed.

    Available expanded memory . . . . . . .    512 KB

    LIM/EMS version . . . . . . . . . . . .    4.0
    Total expanded memory pages . . . . . .    56
    Available expanded memory pages . . . . .  32
    Total handles . . . . . . . . . . . . .    64
    Active handles  . . . . . . . . . . . .    1
    Page frame segment  . . . . . . . . . .    E000 H

    Total upper memory available  . . . . .    95 KB
    Largest Upper Memory Block available  . .  64 KB
    Upper memory starting address . . . . . .  C800 H

EMM386 Active.
```

Figure 6-6. *A system with available upper memory.*

Note: *This trick will work only when you direct the EMM386.EXE device driver to simulate expanded memory and you use the ram option. If you use the noems option, a page frame isn't created.*

SUMMARY

You can take advantage of upper memory blocks (UMBs) to load device drivers and memory-resident programs into the upper memory area, leaving more conventional memory for your memory-hungry applications.

■ UMBs are created by three commands in your CONFIG.SYS file:

```
device=c:\dos\himem.sys
dos=high,umb
device=c:\dos\emm386.exe noems
```

■ The command that loads the EMM386.EXE device driver must have either the ram or noems option after it to create the UMBs. If you specify the ram option, EMM386.EXE uses extended memory to simulate expanded memory in addition to creating the UMBs. If the noems option is specified, the UMBs are created but EMM386.EXE does not simulate any expanded memory. (noems is the option to use for running Windows.)

■ After you've created UMBs, you can use the Devicehigh and Loadhigh commands to load device drivers and memory-resident programs into the UMBs.

■ The Devicehigh command loads device drivers into UMBs. Devicehigh is used exactly like the Device command in a CONFIG.SYS file.

■ If your computer locks up after loading a device driver into a UMB, use Devicehigh's size option to specify the minimum amount of free memory the device driver must have to be loaded into a UMB.

■ A good strategy to take with loading device drivers into UMBs is to load the larger ones first.

■ The Loadhigh command loads memory-resident programs into UMBs. You simply place Loadhigh, or LH, in front of the command that loads the memory-resident program, either in AUTOEXEC.BAT or on the command line.

■ On some computers, an extra 64-KB UMB can be created by moving the page frame to segment E000. To do this, use the frame=e000 option before the ram option in the command that loads the EMM386.EXE device driver in CONFIG.SYS.

Chapter 7

Using a RAM Disk and a Disk Cache

Don't get caught thinking "I bought too much memory. I have nothing to do with it." Rest assured: There's always something you can use extra memory for. Even if your applications use only a small portion of memory, you can put the remainder to good use by creating a RAM disk or a disk cache to enhance the speed of disk operations.

WHAT IS A RAM DISK?

A RAM disk is an area of memory that behaves like a very fast disk drive. You don't need special hardware to install a RAM disk. You need only a device driver that convinces DOS to treat a portion of memory as if it were a disk drive.

You can use a RAM disk as you would any other type of disk drive: You can copy files to and from it, give others access to it over a network, make subdirectories on it, and so on. You can't, however, format a RAM disk.

The biggest advantage of using a RAM disk is speed. Because a RAM disk is an area of memory, it is many times faster than a real disk drive—even faster than a hard disk. And because it has no moving parts, a RAM disk can save wear and tear on your real disk drives.

A RAM disk has two disadvantages. The first disadvantage is that it uses some of your computer's memory. A 512-KB RAM disk uses 512 KB of memory (although this memory can be conventional, expanded, or extended memory).

The second disadvantage is that a RAM disk is volatile. If you shut the computer off, if you reboot the computer, or if the power goes off, information in the RAM disk is lost. This might not seem to be a big disadvantage—until you've lost a file that you've worked on for hours.

If you have extra memory and are careful about backing up important data on a floppy disk or a hard disk, the advantages of a RAM disk far outweigh the disadvantages.

INSTALLING THE RAMDRIVE.SYS DEVICE DRIVER

The DOS 5 device driver that creates a RAM disk is RAM-DRIVE.SYS. You can create as many RAM disks as your computer's memory can handle. Simply load the RAMDRIVE.SYS device driver once for each RAM disk you want to create. The RAMDRIVE.SYS device driver is loaded with the Device command in your CONFIG.SYS file. The format is

```
device=c:\dos\ramdrive.sys [size[sector[entries]]] [/e:/a]
```

You must specify the correct path to RAMDRIVE.SYS. In this example, RAMDRIVE.SYS is assumed to be in your C:\DOS subdirectory.

size is the size of the RAM disk in kilobytes. Values for *size* range from 16 through 4096 for a 16-KB through 4-MB RAM disk. When *size* isn't specified, a 64-KB RAM disk is created.

sector is the size of the RAM disk's sectors in bytes. (A sector is a unit of disk storage. A small sector size is good for storing small files, and a large sector size is good for storing large files.) Values for *sector* can be 128, 256, or the default of 512. (512 is the standard size of sectors on floppies and hard disks.) You must specify a *size* value if you specify a *sector* value.

entries indicates the number of directory entries RAMDRIVE.SYS will create in the RAM disk's root directory. (A directory entry is a place where DOS stores filenames. If you specify 64 for entries, DOS can store 64 files in the root directory of the RAM disk.) Values for *entries* range from 2 through 1024, with a default of 64. You must specify *size* and *sector* values if you specify an *entries* value.

The /e or /a switches (use one or the other—not both) direct RAMDRIVE.SYS to create the RAM disk in extended or expanded memory. If these switches are omitted, the RAM disk is created in conventional memory.

The letter DOS assigns to the RAM disk will always be one letter higher than the last drive in your computer. If you have drives A, B, and C, the RAM disk will be drive D. If you have drives through the letter H, the RAM disk will be drive I.

You can create as many RAM disks as your computer's memory will support. Each RAM disk will be given the next-highest letter in the alphabet, up through Z. (Each drive letter uses about 80 bytes of conventional memory.)

Note: If you do go beyond E with the RAM disk letters, use the Last-drive command to set the highest drive letter for DOS. For example, the command lastdrive=z *in your CONFIG.SYS file will let you have disk drives up through letter Z. Each additional drive uses about 80 bytes of conventional memory.*

Creating a RAM Disk

Creating a RAM disk is painless. For the memory it uses, the benefits to your computer can be great—especially if you have enough memory for a RAM disk over 1 MB in size. For practice, create a 64-KB RAM disk in conventional, extended, or expanded memory—whichever type of memory your computer has. Installing a RAM disk is easier than loading a device driver or memory-resident program, so we'll be modifying the CONFIG.SYS and AUTOEXEC.BAT files on your hard disk.

First decide what type of memory the RAM disk will use. Use the Mem command to check the amount of extended, expanded, and

conventional memory available on your computer. For example, on
my computer, I see the following:

```
655360 bytes total conventional memory
655360 bytes available to MS-DOS
606288 largest executable program size

917504 bytes total EMS memory
524288 bytes free EMS memory

1310720 bytes total contiguous extended memory
      0 bytes available contiguous extended memory
 589824 bytes available XMS memory
        MS-DOS resident in High Memory Area
```

My computer has 524,288 bytes of expanded memory and 589,824
bytes of extended memory. A 64-KB RAM disk can be created in any
type of memory on my computer, but I'll create a RAM disk in extended memory because I don't run any applications that use extended memory on this computer. Make a similar decision for your
own computer. If you don't have enough extended or expanded
memory, simply use conventional memory for this test. (At only 64
KB, it's not much lost memory.)

Use the DOS 5 Edit program to insert the following line at the bottom
of your CONFIG.SYS file:

```
device=c:\dos\ramdrive.sys /e
```

Specify the correct path for RAMDRIVE.SYS; unless you've moved
RAMDRIVE.SYS, it's in your DOS subdirectory, which should be
specified after *device=*. In this example, the C:\DOS subdirectory is
assumed.

The above command creates a 64-KB RAM disk in extended
memory. If you have expanded memory to spare, add the /a switch to
the end of the command instead of the /e switch; if you'd rather
create the RAM disk in conventional memory, leave off the /e and /a
switches.

On my computer, I've used the /e switch to create the 64-KB RAM
disk in extended memory. Incidentally, because my computer loads

several device drivers, here is the order in which device drivers are loaded in my CONFIG.SYS file:

```
devicehigh=c:\dos\himem.sys
dos=high,umb
devicehigh=c:\dos\emm386.exe
devicehigh=c:\mouse\mouse.sys /c1
devicehigh=c:\dos\ansi.sys
devicehigh=c:\dos\ramdrive.sys /e
```

Save your own CONFIG.SYS file, exit to DOS, and then reboot your computer.

As your computer boots, you'll see the RAMDRIVE.SYS startup message displayed:

```
Microsoft RAMDrive version 3.06 virtual disk D:
    Disk size: 64k
    Sector size: 512 bytes
    Allocation unit: 1 sectors
    Directory entries: 64
```

On my computer, the RAM disk is drive D. (Your RAM disk might be assigned a different letter; watch the RAMDRIVE.SYS startup message to find out which drive letter DOS assigns to your RAM disk.) Although the RAM disk doesn't contain any files yet, it does have the volume label MS-RAMDRIVE.

Confirm the RAM disk's size with the Chkdsk command. Type

```
chkdsk d:
```

(This command assumes your RAM disk is drive D. If your RAM disk isn't drive D, use its drive letter instead of D.) The output of the Chkdsk command will look like this:

```
Volume MS-RAMDRIVE created 02-27-1991 12:00a

    62464 bytes total disk space
    62464 bytes available on disk

      512 bytes in each allocation unit
      122 total allocation units on disk
      122 available allocation units on disk

    655360 total bytes memory
    622752 bytes free
```

Note: The memory information provided by the Chkdsk command is limited to conventional memory. To obtain information about expanded and extended memory as well, use the Mem command.

A 64-KB RAM disk isn't useful for much (although a 16-KB RAM disk is wonderful for storing batch files—more on that later). For best performance, you should specify a RAM disk as large as the amount of free extended or expanded memory you have, up to 4 MB. On my computer, that's about 512 KB of extended memory. The command to create a 512-KB RAM disk in extended memory is

```
device=c:\dos\ramdrive.sys 512 /e
```

After I add this command to my CONFIG.SYS file and reboot my computer, the Mem command reports that I have only 65,536 bytes (64 KB) of free extended memory left—but that's okay because no applications on my computer use extended memory. In fact, I could have created a 576-KB RAM disk in extended memory.

Loading RAMDRIVE.SYS High

Because you've learned to be a conscientious DOS 5 memory user, you're probably wondering how much of your precious conventional memory the RAMDRIVE.SYS device driver is using. The RAMDRIVE.SYS device driver can be loaded into a UMB to free conventional memory. As was discussed in Chapter 6, before loading any device driver into a UMB you should first use the Mem /c command to check the size of the device driver. The Mem /c command reveals the size of the RAMDRIVE.SYS device driver:

```
RAMDRIVE          1184      ( 1.2K)        4A0
```

RAMDRIVE.SYS is using only 1184 bytes of memory (about 1.2 KB).

Note: When you load the RAMDRIVE.SYS device driver into a UMB, you load only the device driver—not the RAM disk itself, which can be in conventional, extended, or expanded memory. Also, no matter how many RAM disks you create or how big the RAM disks are, each RAMDRIVE.SYS device driver takes up about 1.2 KB of memory.

To load the RAMDRIVE.SYS device driver into an upper memory block, use the following command in your CONFIG.SYS file:

```
devicehigh=c:\dos\ramdrive.sys
```

Of course, indicate the proper path (C:\DOS is assumed above), and add whatever switches you need (/e to use extended memory; /a to use expanded memory). Also, to use the memory available in UMBs most efficiently, load device drivers in order from largest to smallest. For example, the sizes of the MOUSE.SYS, ANSI.SYS, and RAMDRIVE.SYS device drivers are as follows:

```
RAMDRIVE       1184    ( 1.2K)     4A0
MOUSE         14816    ( 14.5K)    39E0
ANSI           4192    ( 4.1K)     1060
```

Since MOUSE.SYS is the largest device driver, load it into a UMB first. Load the ANSI.SYS device driver next, and then load the RAMDRIVE.SYS device driver.

RAM Disk Strategy

To run an application from a RAM disk, you must first copy the application to the RAM disk. But when you've finished running the application, you must copy any new or changed data back to the hard disk for permanent storage. Two simple rules cover this:

- Copy disk-intensive applications to the RAM disk, and then run the application from the RAM disk.

- When you've finished running the application, copy any new or changed data files (a word processor document, program source code, a spreadsheet file, and so on) from the RAM disk to the hard disk.

If you're good with DOS, use batch files to copy the application to a RAM disk, and then run the application from the RAM disk. Advanced DOS users typically use batch files to run most applications anyway. Adding a few commands to copy applications to the RAM disk—and then to copy new or changed data files back to the hard disk when you've finished with the applications—takes only two more commands in the batch file.

Things to Do with a RAM Disk

I once read with great enthusiasm a magazine article that purportedly gave away speed-boosting secrets for 100 DOS applications. Allow me to summarize it for you: *Use a RAM disk.* For applications that couldn't benefit from a RAM disk, the author had the following suggestion: *Add expanded memory.* (And they paid this guy!)

A RAM disk is most helpful with the following types of programs:

- **Applications that frequently access a disk drive.** Any disk-intensive program will benefit from a RAM disk. (A compiler is a good example.) If the hard-disk light frequently flashes while an application is running, copy the entire application to a RAM disk, and run the application from the RAM disk. (We'll see how to do this later.)

- **Applications with overlay files.** Many applications are too big to fit into conventional memory. One common solution to this problem is to break up an application into several smaller modules called *overlays*. Each overlay contains instructions that handle a specific task. For example, a word processor might have an overlay for saving and loading documents, an overlay for checking spelling, an overlay for printing, and so on.

The word processor has a main unit that always stays in memory. This unit handles normal tasks—inserting and deleting text, cutting and pasting, and so on. But when you do something special—like printing—the main unit must load the printing overlay from disk and transfer control to the printing overlay. The printing overlay performs the print operation, exits (freeing the memory it was using), and returns control to the main unit of the word processor.

This solution has one disadvantage: The delay that occurs while an overlay loads from disk can be annoying. That's why running this type of application from a RAM disk is such an improvement: Overlay files load much faster from a RAM disk than from an actual disk drive.

- **Graphics applications.** Sometimes large graphics images can't be stored in memory all at once. Some graphics applications will save and load pieces of the image on disk as you manipulate the image. If your graphics application can load and save these pieces in a RAM disk, the application can work faster with large images.

A RAM disk isn't helpful for the following types of programs and situations:

- **Applications that rarely access a disk.** RAM disks are beneficial only to programs that load or save information on disk.

- **Copy-protected software.** Although few applications are copy protected anymore, those that are probably won't run from a RAM disk. (This category includes computer games, which tend to be copy protected more than other applications.)

- **Power failures.** When the power goes off, any information in the RAM disk is lost.

If you're *really* good with DOS, you can include the commands to copy applications to a RAM disk in your AUTOEXEC.BAT file. The drawback to this is that it can take a long time for your computer to boot. An example is provided later in this chapter.

The following sections give examples of using a RAM disk in various situations and for various purposes.

Disk-Intensive Applications

Any disk-intensive application will run faster from a RAM disk. Most word processing programs are very disk intensive, so as an example, I'll show you the steps necessary to run Microsoft Word version 5.5 from a RAM disk.

First you need to add a command to your CONFIG.SYS file to create a RAM disk. Microsoft Word 5.5 and its support files require a lot of storage space, so you'll need a big RAM disk. (I recommend a 4-MB RAM disk.) Use the DOS 5 Edit program to add the following command to your CONFIG.SYS file:

```
devicehigh=c:\dos\ramdrive.sys 4096 /e
```

This command creates a 4-MB RAM disk in extended memory (the /a switch creates the RAM disk in expanded memory) and assumes that RAMDRIVE.SYS is in the C:\DOS subdirectory. If RAMDRIVE.SYS is not in the C:\DOS subdirectory, specify the correct path.

Save the CONFIG.SYS file, and reboot your computer. Watch for the RAMDRIVE.SYS startup message to determine what drive letter DOS assigns to the RAM disk.

Now you need to add commands to your AUTOEXEC.BAT file that copy the Word 5.5 files to your RAM disk. Use the DOS 5 Edit program to add these commands to the end of your AUTOEXEC.BAT file:

```
md d:\word
xcopy c:\word\*.* d:\word /s
```

This example makes two assumptions. The first assumption is that your RAM disk is drive D. If your RAM disk is not drive D, specify the proper drive letter instead. The second assumption is that the Word 5.5 files are in the C:\WORD subdirectory. If the Word 5.5 files are in a different subdirectory, specify the correct path.

You also need to place the Word 5.5 files in your computer's search path. If you already have a Path command in AUTOEXEC.BAT, add the D:\WORD subdirectory to it. Otherwise, add the following command to your AUTOEXEC.BAT file:

```
path=c:\dos;d:\word
```

Again, this assumes your RAM disk is drive D. If your RAM disk is not drive D, specify the proper drive letter instead.

Save AUTOEXEC.BAT and reboot your computer. After the computer boots, load Word 5.5 by typing WORD at the DOS prompt. You'll be impressed with how fast Word 5.5 loads and runs. Be sure to copy documents you saved in the RAM disk to the hard disk when you exit Word 5.5.

Temporary and Overflow Files

Some applications use a subdirectory for temporary or overflow files. For example, Windows lets you specify a directory for temporary files using the environment variable TEMP. Why not specify the root directory of your RAM disk? You'll notice a significant speed increase while running Windows. (More hints on optimizing Windows' performance are given in the next chapter.)

Ventura Publisher and other large applications that work with lots of data let you specify a RAM disk for overflow files. WordPerfect's Setup command tells WordPerfect where to save temporary and timed backup files, so why not use a RAM disk for these files? You can copy the spelling and thesaurus files to a RAM disk and then use WordPerfect's Setup command to tell WordPerfect to look for the spelling and thesaurus files in the RAM disk. A spelling check will go much faster when the dictionary is in a RAM disk.

Many applications have a command that tells the application where to store temporary and overflow files. For optimal performance, create a RAM disk specifically for these temporary files, making it at least 1 MB in size.

Optimizing for Batch Files

Anyone who uses DOS should consider batch files as a productivity booster. On my computer, *all* applications are run through batch files, which are all located in a batch file subdirectory *in a RAM disk*. The batch files are all created and stored in the BATCH subdirectory on the hard disk. When my computer boots, my AUTOEXEC.BAT file creates a BATCH subdirectory in my RAM disk (drive D on my computer), copies the batch files there, and then places that directory in my computer's search path. The following three lines in my AUTOEXEC.BAT file do the job:

```
md d:\batch
xcopy c:\batch\*.* d:\batch
path=d:\batch;c:\dos;c:\util
```

If you want to really maximize performance, create a unique RAM disk for your batch files. Make the RAM disk small and the sector size small because batch files don't require much space. But specify quite a few directory entries in the root directory of the RAM disk. The following command in your CONFIG.SYS file would work well:

```
device=c:\dos\ramdrive.sys 16 128 128 /e
```

This command creates a 16-KB RAM disk in extended memory with 128-byte sectors and room for 128 directory entries in the root directory. Then add a command to your AUTOEXEC.BAT file to copy all your batch files from the hard disk to the RAM disk, and add the RAM disk to your computer's search path.

It's important to remember that the batch files are in the RAM disk. If you add or edit a batch file, do so on the hard disk, and then copy the new batch file to your RAM disk.

The Download Directory

If you use your computer for telecommunications, you can *download* software from national online networks, local computers, or the office. If so, using a RAM disk as the download directory saves time. Additionally, since most downloaded software is in a compressed format, decompressing the files in the RAM disk will go faster as well.

Demo Programs

In the same vein as downloading programs, it pays sometimes to install demo software in a RAM disk. Run the program from the RAM disk. If you like the program, copy it to your hard disk. If you don't like the program, it will automatically be discarded when you turn your computer off. The only drawback occurs if a demo insists on rebooting your computer to run itself. When that happens, the RAM disk is erased, and the demo is gone.

USING A DISK CACHE

Disk caches and RAM disks are almost always mentioned in the same breath. True, they both take advantage of memory to improve your computer's performance. But that's about where the similarity ends.

A disk cache (pronounced *cash*) is basically a large disk buffer, a storage place in memory for information read from disk. When DOS reads information from disk, a copy of the information is kept in the cache, from which it can be quickly read again, as necessary. Reading the information from the disk cache is much faster than reading it from disk.

Although a cache saves you from performing an unnecessary number of disk reads, it doesn't affect how information is written to a disk. Information is always written directly to disk, ensuring that not even a power failure results in lost information.

Note: Caches can have a drawback: They cause some applications to lock up the computer. No information is lost, but you have to reboot.

Using the SMARTDRV.SYS Disk Cache

The disk cache that comes with DOS 5 is the SMARTDRV.SYS device driver. To install SMARTDRV.SYS, insert the following command in your CONFIG.SYS file:

```
device=c:\dos\smartdrv.sys [max[min]][/a]
```

Be sure to specify the proper path; in this example, the C:\DOS subdirectory is assumed.

max reflects the maximum size for the cache in kilobytes. Values for *max* range from 128 through 8192 for a 128-KB through 8-MB cache. If *max* is omitted, a 256-KB cache is created. If there's not enough memory to create a cache of the specified size, SMARTDRV.SYS creates a smaller cache, using whatever memory is available.

min reflects the minimum size for the cache in kilobytes. Microsoft Windows can reduce the size of the cache to recover memory for its own use. When Windows exits, it releases the memory back to the cache. Values for *min* should be less than *max*, all the way down to 0. The default is 0. You must specify a value for *max* if you specify a value for *min*. A good combination for Windows (if you have enough memory) is to set *max* to 1024 and *min* to 256.

The /a switch tells the SMARTDRV.SYS device driver to create the cache using expanded memory. If /a is omitted, the cache is created using extended memory.

Why specify maximum and minimum values? Convenience. These values provide a boundary around which Windows can manipulate the size of the cache as necessary.

Creating the Disk Cache

One cache will serve all your needs, caching all hard disks in your computer. A good maximum size to specify is the default, 256 KB. If memory is tight, specify a smaller value; even a 128-KB cache is useful. Follow these steps.

1. Edit your CONFIG.SYS file. Insert the following command at the end of the file:

```
device=c:\dos\smartdrv.sys
```

Specify the proper path for the SMARTDRV.SYS device driver. (This example assumes SMARTDRV.SYS is in the C:\DOS subdirectory.) Place the maximum size of the disk cache after *smartdrv.sys*, followed by an optional minimum size if you're running Windows. (1024 and 256 are good values for *max* and *min* when running Windows.) In this example, the cache will be created using extended memory. If you want to create the cache using expanded memory, place an /a switch at the end of the command.

An example of creating a 256-KB cache using expanded memory would be:

```
device=c:\dos\smartdrv.sys 256 /a
```

2. Save CONFIG.SYS, exit to DOS, and reboot your computer.

When the computer boots, you'll see the SMARTDRV.SYS startup message displayed:

```
Microsoft SMARTDrive Disk Cache version 3.13
    Cache size: 256K in Extended Memory
    Room for 30 tracks of 17 sectors each
    Minimum cache size will be OK
```

In this example, a 256-KB cache is created using extended memory; if you specify a different size or memory type, this will be reflected in the SMARTDRV.SYS startup message.

That's it! You should notice immediate improvement. As a test, do a few Dir commands in a row, and notice their increased speed.

Loading SMARTDRV.SYS High

Like any other device driver, SMARTDRV.SYS can be loaded into a UMB (and *should* be—it takes up 13 KB of valuable memory).

To load the SMARTDRV.SYS device driver into an upper memory block, simply use the Devicehigh command instead of the Device command in CONFIG.SYS. But carefully note the size of SMARTDRV.SYS. If you're loading device drivers in order from largest to smallest, be sure you get the order right. Earlier in this chapter, you saw the size of some other device drivers:

```
RAMDRIVE          1184     ( 1.2K)        4A0
MOUSE            14816     ( 14.5K)       39E0
ANSI             4192     ( 4.1K)        1060
```

If you're going to load device drivers into UMBs in order from largest to smallest, MOUSE.SYS comes first, followed by SMART-DRV.SYS, ANSI.SYS, and RAMDRIVE.SYS. Edit your CONFIG.SYS file accordingly, listing the files in that order. For example

```
devicehigh=c:\mouse\mouse.sys /cl
devicehigh=c:\dos\smartdrv.sys
devicehigh=c:\dos\ansi.sys
devicehigh=c:\dos\ramdrive.sys /e
```

Save CONFIG.SYS, exit to DOS, and then reboot your computer. (If your computer locks up after loading SMARTDRV.SYS high, load it low instead.)

The Fastopen Command

DOS 3.3 came with a file location caching program called Fastopen. Each time you accessed a file, DOS would search for the subdirectory that contained the file and then search that subdirectory itself. Using the Fastopen command, DOS would keep track (in memory) of the locations of files and subdirectories you accessed. Any additional access to those files and subdirectories was much quicker because DOS wouldn't need to search for the location of the file or subdirectory.

Fastopen only stored locations of files and subdirectories; no data from disk was stored. If you don't have enough memory to load the SMARTDRV.SYS device driver, you can use the Fastopen command instead. My personal advice is to use a cache if at all possible.

OTHER OPTIMIZATION HINTS

If getting your computer to run as fast as possible has become your obsession, take advantage of the following hints to make your computer run faster. Not every hint involves memory, but each one contributes to your computer's efficiency.

- **Perform regular cleanup and file maintenance.** It's always a good idea to remove unneeded or temporary files from your hard disk. A good disk utility can help in this regard.

- **Clean up unallocated clusters on the hard disk.** Type *chkdsk /f* at the DOS prompt. The Chkdsk command, with its /f switch, looks for lost chains and clusters on disk. Those are file fragments typically left behind when a file wasn't closed properly. This can happen when you turn the computer off without exiting an application (or when a power failure occurs). The Chkdsk command will remove these fragments, making your disk more efficient.

- **Compress your hard disk.** Over time, files stored on disk tend to get broken into pieces and scattered all over the disk. (These are known as *fragmented files*.) Fragmented files take longer to load because the read/write head must be moved to read each fragment of the file.

  You can buy third-party programs that solve this problem. These programs basically copy each file to a contiguous, empty area on the disk and then erase the original file. Some programs are more elaborate than others, freeing unused disk space and optionally changing the order of files so that frequently used files load faster than infrequently used files.

- **Set up a print buffer or spooler.** A print buffer is an area of memory used to temporarily store a file you send to the printer. The computer sends the file to the printer while letting you run an application. Although this doesn't speed up the printer, it does free you to proceed with other activities while the file is being printed.

A print spooler is a program that saves (on disk) files to be printed and then prints the files out while you can run another application. Both the print buffer and the print spooler require special software and some unused memory. The drawback is that some are incompatible with other applications (especially applications that ignore the standard DOS printing functions).

SUMMARY

After you have extra memory, two good ways to put it to use are as a RAM disk and a disk cache. Both a RAM disk and a disk cache use memory to improve your computer's performance: A RAM disk operates like an extremely fast disk drive, and a disk cache speeds up read operations on your hard disks.

■ A RAM disk is part of your computer's memory that behaves like a disk drive. The RAMDRIVE.SYS device driver fools DOS into thinking that the RAM disk is really another disk drive. Because that disk is in memory, it works much faster than a real disk drive.

■ The RAMDRIVE.SYS device driver that comes with DOS 5 lets you create a RAM disk from 16 KB to 4 MB in size, in conventional, extended, or expanded memory. You can create as many RAM disks as you like, limited by the amount of memory in your computer.

■ The RAMDRIVE.SYS device driver can be loaded into a UMB using the Devicehigh command. But note that only the device driver—not the RAM disk itself—will be loaded into a UMB.

■ You can run any disk-intensive application from a RAM disk to greatly improve the application's performance. However, if you create any new data files on the RAM disk, always copy them to the hard disk before turning your computer off.

■ A disk cache is a part of memory used to store information read from disk. When that same information needs to be read again, it's read from the disk cache instead of from disk. The end result is a faster computer.

- The disk cache that comes with DOS 5 is SMARTDRV.SYS. SMARTDRV.SYS can create a disk cache between 128 KB and 8 MB in size. Realistically, any size disk cache will improve disk performance—even on the fastest hard disks.

Chapter 8

Preparing for Microsoft Windows

Microsoft Windows is pretty to look at, fun to use, gives your PC graphics muscle, and exploits the full power of your machine.

It also requires a lot of memory.

DOS 5 has been tailored to work well with Windows, giving you much more free conventional memory for your applications.

In this chapter, you'll learn how to use DOS 5 to make Windows run more efficiently. You'll also benefit from specific tips that help you get the most from Windows. Most of these suggestions work best if you're running Windows on a '386-based computer that has 1 MB (or more) of extended memory, although many of the suggestions here will help 80286-based computers even when they're not running Windows.

USING DOS 5 AND WINDOWS

Windows 3.0 has three modes of operation: 386 enhanced mode (for '386-based computers with at least 1 MB of extended memory), standard mode (for 80286-based computers), and real mode. Although '386-based and 80286-based computers can run Windows in a lesser mode, you usually want to run Windows in the most powerful mode possible on your computer. For 80286-based and '386-based computers, this means that your computer needs plenty of extended memory available, plus as much free conventional memory as possible.

115

Setting Up Memory

The first concern is extended memory: Windows wants a lot of it. You need at least 384 KB of extended memory on an 80286-based or '386-based computer to run Windows in standard mode; and you need 1 MB of extended memory (2 MB total memory) on a '386-based computer to run Windows in 386 enhanced mode. In standard or 386 enhanced mode, Windows doesn't want to use expanded memory.

When you run the Windows Setup program, it automatically installs the HIMEM.SYS device driver in the CONFIG.SYS file on 80286-based or '386-based computers:

```
device=c:\windows\himem.sys
```

Coincidentally, that's the first step required for DOS 5 to get the most from memory: HIMEM.SYS manages the use of extended memory. Furthermore, HIMEM.SYS gives 80286-based and '386-based computers access to the high memory area (HMA).

Note: The HMA is most useful as a storage area for part of DOS. (See Chapter 5.)

If your CONFIG.SYS file contains expanded memory manager device drivers, the Windows Setup program will ask you to remove them. You should do so to get the best performance from Windows on an 80286-based or '386-based computer. (It's not that Windows is incompatible with expanded memory; Windows can use expanded memory and will take advantage of it. It's simply that, on an 80286-based or '386-based computer, Windows works best with extended memory.)

After all device drivers and memory-resident programs have been loaded into UMBs, the only extra thing you can do to get better performance from Windows is to add more extended memory to your computer. On a '386-based computer, 2 MB of memory is barely enough to run Windows in 386 enhanced mode. To get the best performance from Windows, be sure your computer has at least 4 MB of extended memory. In fact, that will give you enough memory to create a disk cache and a RAM disk. (See Chapter 7.)

Next you'll want to clear out conventional memory. Follow the procedure described in Chapter 5. Although Windows needs only 300 KB of conventional memory, you want to have as much free as possible for running your DOS applications under Windows. In the olden days, Windows gave you about 536 KB of free conventional memory for DOS applications. But by loading device drivers and memory-resident programs into UMBs (as described in Chapters 5 and 6), you can have up to 615 KB (or more) of free conventional memory when running Windows.

Setting Up AUTOEXEC.BAT

Now that you've structured the computer's memory to work with Windows, you can make two changes to the AUTOEXEC.BAT file. These changes allow AUTOEXEC.BAT to start Windows when your computer boots:

1. Add your Windows subdirectory to the Path command. (This might have already been done by the Windows Setup program.)

2. Place the Win command at the end of your AUTOEXEC.BAT file.

   Note: If you have an EGA graphics card and monitor, be sure the command device=c:\dos\ega.sys *is in your CONFIG.SYS file. (And be sure to specify the correct path for EGA.SYS.) It's okay to load the EGA.SYS device driver into a UMB.*

3. Save AUTOEXEC.BAT, and then reboot your computer. Your computer will boot and then load Windows.

4. After Windows has loaded, go into the Program Manager if it isn't already open. Drop down the Help menu, and select the last item, About Program Manager.... You will see a dialog box similar to Figure 8-1.

In the About dialog box you'll see several important items of information. First is the mode Windows is running in. In Figure 8-1, *386 enhanced mode* is displayed. Other modes are the *standard mode* and the *real mode*. Confirm that Windows is running in the mode you expected, the best mode possible on your computer.

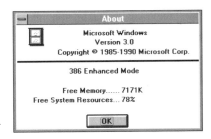

Figure 8-1. *The About dialog box.*

If you don't see the mode you expected, you must make some adjustments. If you have a '386-based computer and have prepared it as described in Chapters 5 and 6, yet you see real or standard mode displayed, you should edit your CONFIG.SYS file and confirm that EMM386.EXE isn't using extended memory to simulate expanded memory. Also, you might try reducing the size of your disk cache. On a 2-MB '386-based computer with a disk cache, Windows might not have enough memory to run in 386 enhanced mode. Also be sure you have enough extended memory installed: Windows comes up in a lesser mode when an 80286-based or '386-based computer doesn't have enough extended memory for standard mode or 386 enhanced mode.

The amount of *Free Memory* reflected in the About dialog box might be more memory than is in your computer. Don't panic. Windows is telling you how much free conventional, extended, and *virtual* memory is available. Windows provides virtual memory by using the hard disk to simulate extra RAM.

To see how much memory is installed in your computer, use the Mem command:

1. Close the About dialog box, and double-click on the DOS Prompt icon in the Main group.

2. At the DOS prompt, type *mem*. You'll see something like the following:

```
 655360 bytes total conventional memory
 655360 bytes available to MS-DOS
 615584 largest executable program size

1671168 bytes total EMS memory
 311296 bytes free EMS memory

1310720 bytes total contiguous extended memory
      0 bytes available contiguous extended memory
 937984 bytes available XMS memory
        MS-DOS resident in High Memory Area
```

On my computer, I have 615,584 bytes of unused conventional memory—a whopping amount. Of course, it's overshadowed by the 1.6 MB of available EMS memory. (Windows is using extended memory to simulate expanded memory.)

3. Type *exit* to close the DOS shell and return to Windows.

The WINA20.386 File

When you ran the DOS 5 Setup program, it placed a file named WINA20.386 in the root directory of your hard disk. If you don't have a '386-based computer, feel free to delete the WINA20.386 file.

As we saw in Chapter 5, the HMA is accessed by enabling address line 20 on 80286 and '386 microprocessors. WINA20.386 resolves any conflicts when DOS 5 and Windows (in 386 enhanced mode) both try to access the HMA.

OPTIMIZING WINDOWS PERFORMANCE

When you're trying to optimize Windows performance, you're simply dealing with a question of resource management. Disk storage and memory are the two main resources you can manipulate to give Windows more speed and power. Of course, you could always throw money at the problem and buy an i486-based computer with a huge, fast, hard disk and megabytes of RAM. But because you're probably required to operate within a budget, you must make the most of what you already have.

First upgrade to DOS 5, and free as much conventional memory as possible, as described in Chapters 5 and 6. After that, the Windows optimization strategy becomes more specific, depending on your computer's resources.

The following sections list various steps you can take to get the most from Windows. Practice with several configurations and options—especially if memory is low—before creating your ideal Windows setup.

Using SMARTDRV.SYS

Under most circumstances, the Windows Setup program installs the SMARTDRV.SYS device driver in your CONFIG.SYS file, assigning a disk cache size based on the amount of memory in your computer.

Because Windows provides virtual memory by using your hard disk to simulate RAM, having a large disk cache will boost Windows performance. But if your computer has memory to spare, consider devoting most of it to a RAM disk and storing Windows program and temporary files there instead. (This topic is covered later.) An adequate size for the disk cache would then be about 128 KB to 512 KB (more if your computer has the memory). The following line in your CONFIG.SYS file creates a 256-KB disk cache, with a minimum size of 128 KB—ample for most Windows configurations:

```
devicehigh=c:\dos\smartdrv.sys 256 128
```

Note: The SMARTDRV.SYS disk cache device driver is covered in detail in Chapter 7.

When memory is tight, say on a 2-MB computer, specifying too large a size for SMARTDRV.SYS might force Windows to run in a lesser mode (standard mode instead of 386 enhanced mode, for example).

If Windows is running in a lesser mode than you expect, try specifying a 128-KB cache with a 0 minimum size:

```
devicehigh=c:\dos\smartdrv.sys 128
```

Refer to Chapter 7 for more information on the SMARTDRV.SYS device driver.

Using RAMDRIVE.SYS

If your computer has memory to spare, devote most of it to a RAM disk instead of the disk cache. Putting any disk-intensive programs in the RAM disk is a definite productivity booster, particularly when you're running Windows.

To set up the RAM disk, use the RAMDRIVE.SYS device driver. For example, the following command in CONFIG.SYS creates a 2-MB RAM disk:

```
devicehigh=c:\dos\ramdrive.sys 2048 /e
```

The /e switch creates the RAM disk in extended memory. Refer to Chapter 7 for more information about the RAMDRIVE.SYS device driver.

After the RAM disk is created, you can start placing Windows program files there. But you must first tell Windows to use the RAM disk for temporary files. Add the following command to your AUTOEXEC.BAT file:

```
set temp=d:\
```

This command assumes that your RAM disk is drive D. If necessary, substitute the proper drive letter for your RAM disk. Note that DOS 5 also uses the TEMP environment variable to determine where to store its own temporary files, so using a RAM disk for temporary files improves both Windows and DOS 5 performance.

You can transfer Windows program files into the RAM disk and run them from there. The only drawback is that you need a huge RAM disk to be successful. If your computer has enough memory for a 3-MB RAM disk (and memory is only money), Windows can really scream!

Windows with all its files typically occupies some 6 MB of hard-disk space. Add a few Windows applications and this total can easily hit 10 or 12 MB. But the core of Windows program files occupies only 2 or 3 MB. (A few years ago this whole conversation would have seemed silly; ''only 2 or 3 MB'' is a lot of storage.)

What you encounter at this point is a question of speed versus available memory. It's a trade-off. If you can create a large RAM disk— great! Windows will operate faster. If you cannot create a large RAM disk, consider using a larger disk cache and a small (128-KB) RAM disk for temporary files.

If your computer has the memory for a large RAM disk—or if you can afford to install more memory in your computer—then Windows will run quickly on your computer. For example, suppose your computer has 8 MB of extended memory and you want to create a 4-MB RAM disk. That RAM disk is created in extended memory with the following command:

```
devicehigh=c:\dos\ramdrive.sys 4096 /e
```

To transfer Windows program files to the RAM disk, your AUTOEXEC.BAT file must carry out three tasks. It must

- Create a SYSTEM subdirectory in the RAM disk

- Transfer Windows program files to the SYSTEM subdirectory in the RAM disk

- Put the RAM disk in your computer's search path

The following AUTOEXEC.BAT commands would accomplish these tasks:

```
md d:\system
xcopy c:\windows\system\ *.* d:\system > nul
copy c:\windows\win.com d:\ > nul
xcopy c:\windows\*.grp d:\ > nul
xcopy c:\windows\*.ini d:\ > nul
copy c:\windows\progman.exe d:\ > nul
path d:\;c:\windows;c:\dos
```

Note: *Remember to substitute your RAM disk's drive letter throughout this example. Above, the* > nul *redirection option suppresses the messages produced by the Xcopy and Copy commands.*

If this strategy seems too much for you (after all, not everyone can create a 4-MB RAM disk), consider copying only application files to a RAM disk. Excel for Windows program files occupy less than 2 MB of disk space; Word for Windows program files use only about 1.5 MB of disk space. Both Excel and Word program files could fit on a 4-MB RAM disk to speed them up—again, provided your computer has enough memory for a 4-MB RAM disk. Copy the Excel and Word program files to a RAM disk by using commands in AUTOEXEC.BAT similar to those in the previous example, and then edit the Excel and Word program item properties to tell Windows that Excel and Word are in the RAM disk. (To do this, click on the Excel icon, and then choose Properties from the File menu. Change the command line for Excel to indicate that Excel is in the RAM disk, and then click on OK. Repeat the procedure for Word.)

For additional information on using a RAM disk, refer to Chapter 7.

Using the Swap File

In 386 enhanced mode, Windows creates a temporary swap file on your hard disk. When Windows is low on memory, inactive applications are saved in the swap file, freeing memory for other applications. Essentially, Windows puts an application away on disk, loading it back into memory only when needed.

If you run Windows in 386 enhanced mode, you can create a *permanent swap file* for Windows. A permanent swap file always stays on disk, even when you're not running Windows. And, because it consists of contiguous disk blocks, a permanent swap file is faster than a temporary swap file.

To create a permanent swap file, follow these steps:

1. Quit Windows if you're currently running it. (If you have a utility that allows you to defragment the files on your hard

disk, run it before proceeding to the next step.) At the DOS prompt, start Windows again by typing the following command:

```
win /r swapfile
```

This forces Windows to start in real mode and then run the Swapfile program. (If Windows automatically loads any applications, you'll have to close them before you run the Swapfile program.) The Swapfile dialog box appears, as shown in Figure 8-2.

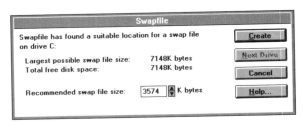

Figure 8-2. *The Swapfile dialog box.*

Note: If you've already created a swap file, you'll be asked whether you want to delete it and create a new one or simply delete it. Select the option to delete the current swap file and create a new one.

The Swapfile program tells you how many bytes are free on the hard disk and the maximum size possible for a swap file. The Swapfile program also recommends a swap file size in the box at the bottom of the dialog box. You can change the size of the swap file: Use the up and down arrows to increase and decrease the size, or simply type in a value. To select a different drive for the swap file, click on the Next Drive button to cycle through all available hard disks in your computer. (Sadly, you cannot specify a RAM disk for the swap file.)

Note: Specify a value for the swap file roughly half of what is suggested. The larger the swap file, the less disk space you'll have for applications.

2. When you're satisfied with the swap file's size, click on the Create button. Swapfile displays a second dialog box indicating that it has created the swap file.

3. Click on OK, and exit Windows and restart it in the 386 enhanced mode.

Cleaning Up CONFIG.SYS

Here are some DOS 5 CONFIG.SYS recommendations for optimizing Windows performance:

- Load the HIMEM.SYS device driver on 80286-based and '386-based computers to give DOS access to the HMA.

- Load part of DOS into the HMA on 80286-based and '386-based computers by using the Dos command.

- Let EMM386.EXE create upper memory blocks on 80286-based and '386-based computers.

- Don't load device drivers you don't need. Better still, put a REM in front of commands that load unneeded device drivers. If you ever need to load one of these device drivers, remove the REM, and reboot your computer.

- When you must load a device driver (such as the Mouse device driver), load the device driver into a UMB. Refer to the instructions in Chapter 6 for more information.

- Use the most recent version of the EMM386.EXE device driver.

- You should generally specify a value of 30 or less for the Files command. (Incidentally, each value greater than 8 uses about 48 bytes of conventional memory.)

- Specify a value of 20 for the Buffers command. If you're using the SMARTDRV.SYS disk cache device driver, specify a value of 10 for the Buffers command. (Note that each buffer uses about 532 bytes of conventional memory.)

- Specify exactly how many drives you have for the Lastdrive command. Be sure to allow for any RAM disks and network drives you'll be using. (Note that each drive you specify above E uses about 80 bytes of conventional memory.)

■ Set the Stacks command as follows: *stacks=0,0.* By default, stacks is set to 9,128 on 80286-based and '386-based computers. Each stack uses a lot of memory; multiply the two values in a Stacks command to see how many bytes are being used. If Windows occasionally locks up your computer, remove the Stacks command.

■ Remove all Install commands (except for SHARE.EXE if you use a network). The Install command loads memory-resident programs that should be loaded into UMBs with the Loadhigh command in AUTOEXEC.BAT.

Cleaning Up AUTOEXEC.BAT

Here are some DOS 5 AUTOEXEC.BAT recommendations for optimizing Windows performance:

■ Don't load unneeded memory-resident programs. In some cases, you'll find equivalent programs that run under Windows. Better still, if the program has a non-memory-resident mode, run it in its own window.

■ Load your necessary memory-resident programs into UMBs using the Loadhigh command. These would include Doskey, Mode, and so on. Refer to Chapter 6.

Hard-Disk Maintenance

Although many users neglect the task, routine hard-disk maintenance is a must for getting the most from your computer:

■ Delete unneeded files, and remove unused subdirectories.

■ Before running Windows, use the Chkdsk /f command to locate and remove lost clusters. (Do not use this command while Windows is running.)

■ Occasionally run a disk defragmentation or compression program to defragment or compress your computer's hard disk. (Do not use this type of program while Windows is running.)

■ After running Windows, delete any Windows temporary files that remain in your root directory. Since these typically begin with the ~ (tilde) character, you can do this with the following command in your AUTOEXEC.BAT file:

```
if exist c:\~*.* del c:\~*.*
```

(Do not use this command while Windows is running.)

■ Back up your hard disk. Although Windows doesn't come with a backup program, DOS does. Better still, third-party backup programs are available. Use them! I perform a full hard-disk backup once a month and a daily backup of all files I work on. Get into this routine! (I became a convert after losing a 90-MB hard disk, paying $1000 for a replacement, *and* wasting three days retyping all my data. Don't you make the same mistake.)

SUMMARY

Windows needn't be a drain on your computer's resources. With the proper configuration, your computer can handle Windows' demands quite easily.

■ To run in standard mode, Windows requires at least 384 KB of extended memory on 80286-based and '386-based computers. Load the DOS 5 HIMEM.SYS device driver to manage your computer's extended memory, and let DOS access the HMA.

■ Free as much conventional memory as possible for Windows by loading part of DOS into the HMA and creating upper memory blocks. To create the UMBs without creating un-needed expanded memory, use EMM386.EXE's noems option.

■ Load your device drivers and memory-resident programs into UMBs with the Devicehigh and the Loadhigh commands, respectively. Load only those device drivers and memory-resident programs that you need.

■ Load the SMARTDRV.SYS disk cache device driver to improve Windows' disk-access time. Give Windows a good-sized disk cache, but devote the majority of any extra memory your computer has to a RAM disk instead.

■ Use the RAMDRIVE.SYS device driver to create a RAM disk, primarily for Windows temporary files. If your computer has enough memory, however, use the RAM disk to store Windows applications or Windows program files. This typically takes a 2-MB or larger RAM disk, but the speed improvement is striking.

■ Clean up your CONFIG.SYS and AUTOEXEC.BAT files. Performing regular hard-disk maintenance is also a good idea.

Chapter 9

Using DOS 5 and Other Memory Managers

This chapter is about four products that augment and extend the memory-management capabilities of DOS 5: 386MAX, MOVE'EM, QEMM-386, and QRAM. They come from two software developers: Quarterdeck Office Systems and Qualitas. And they can do amazing things for *all* IBM-compatible computers—from lowly 8088/8086-based computers up through the latest desk-burner from Compaq.

MEMORY MANAGERS BEYOND DOS

386MAX, MOVE'EM, QEMM-386, and QRAM all offer one or more of the following features:

- An extended memory manager for computers with extended memory

- The ability to simulate expanded memory by using extended memory on a '386-based computer

- An expanded memory manager and backfilling support for 8088/8086-based and 80286-based computers with expanded memory

- The ability to load device drivers and memory-resident programs into UMBs

- The ability to load computer resources into UMBs

- The ability to "steal" video memory to get more conventional memory

Each of these four products is introduced alphabetically in the following four sections. The rest of this chapter provides general hints and memory-management strategies.

386MAX

Qualitas makes 386MAX for '386-based computers with at least 256 KB of extended memory. In addition to a memory manager, 386MAX comes with memory information and usage utilities, as well as a RAM-disk device driver.

A counterpart to 386MAX is BlueMAX, which is specifically designed for IBM PS/2 '386-based computers. BlueMAX takes the Advanced BIOS in those machines and compresses it, freeing up extra upper memory blocks. It also eliminates the seldom-used ROM BASIC in PS/2s, making even more memory available. If you have a PS/2, you should consider getting BlueMAX instead of 386MAX. Otherwise, the two packages function identically. (And both are referred to as *386MAX* in this chapter.)

MOVE'EM

If you have an 8088/8086-based or 80286-based computer and are jealous of what DOS 5 can do for '386-based computers, then MOVE'EM (as well as QRAM) is your revenge.

Qualitas, maker of 386MAX and BlueMAX, offers MOVE'EM as a memory manager and program loader for 80286-based and 8088/8086-based computers with EMS memory installed or computers with the NEAT or AT/386 CHIPSet from Chips and Technologies.

MOVE'EM also comes with several memory-mapping programs, including a program that examines and summarizes the locations and sizes of device drivers and memory-resident programs. It also suggests how to load the device drivers and memory-resident programs into UMBs.

QEMM-386

QEMM-386 is Quarterdeck's expanded memory manager for '386-based computers with at least 1 MB of memory. (If you purchase the DESQview 386 multitasking environment, QEMM is part of the package.)

As part of the QEMM package, you also receive Quarterdeck's Manifest, a computer information program that tells you what's in your computer (both hardware and software) and how your computer's resources are being used.

QRAM

Quarterdeck's memory manager for 8088/8086-based and 80286-based computers is QRAM (pronounced "cram"). QRAM provides extended memory-management capabilities for 80286-based computers, as well as expanded memory-management capabilities for all computers equipped with EMS 4.0–compatible expanded memory. As it is with QEMM-386, Manifest is part of the QRAM package.

How This Chapter Works

Things could get messy here. Consider our subject: DOS 5, plus four memory-management programs for three generations of microprocessors, on computers that might or might not run Windows, plus many other nasty combinations.

Read through the sections that follow, find the information that pertains to your memory manager, and then use the information along with your memory manager's manual.

INSTALLATION AND OPTIMIZATION

If you have already installed a memory manager prior to your DOS 5 upgrade, skip to the section titled "Basic Memory Strategy," which describes how to properly mix DOS 5 and third-party commands to get the most from your computer.

If you are installing a third-party memory manager on your computer, follow these steps:

1. Edit your CONFIG.SYS and AUTOEXEC.BAT files to remove any Devicehigh or Loadhigh commands: In CONFIG.SYS, change Devicehigh back to Device (and remove any size parameters); in AUTOEXEC.BAT, remove Loadhigh or LH from commands that load memory-resident programs.

2. On '386-based computers, remove the command that loads the EMM386.EXE device driver from CONFIG.SYS. On 8088/8086-based computers, put the command that loads your expanded memory manager device driver on the first line of CONFIG.SYS. On 80286-based computers, put the command that loads HIMEM.SYS on the first line of CONFIG.SYS, and the command that loads your expanded memory manager device driver on the second line.

3. Install the third-party memory manager according to its instructions. For now, select all the default options. (Answer *yes* to all the questions.) And be sure to *maximize* or *optimize* your computer when asked.

   Note: For 386MAX, pay careful attention to the information about Windows. If you're using Windows or plan to purchase it in the future, be sure to answer yes *to the question that installs the Windows options.*

After the third-party memory manager is installed, your computer might reboot—maybe even two or three times. If your computer does reboot, some of the DOS commands you already installed might produce errors. That's okay for now; you'll learn how to correct this problem later in this chapter.

Note: Even with all the optimization done by the installation programs, you might still need to do some fine tuning: directing a third-party memory manager to include or exclude parts of memory, adding switches, configuring the memory manager for Windows, and so on. If your computer won't load Windows, refer to your memory manager manual for additional fine-tuning instructions.

Assessing Installation

In the examples that follow, each third-party memory manager was installed on a computer with the following CONFIG.SYS and AUTOEXEC.BAT files.

Standard CONFIG.SYS:

```
device=c:\dos\himem.sys
dos=high
files=30
buffers=20
shell=c:\dos\command.com c:\dos\ /p
stacks=0,0
device=c:\mouse\mouse.sys /c1
```

Standard AUTOEXEC.BAT:

```
@echo off
prompt $p$g
path c:\dos;c:\batch;c:\util
set temp=c:\temp
doskey
```

Each installation program will modify these files as necessary.

Note: Because HIMEM.SYS is incompatible with 8088/8086-based computers, owners of 8088/8086-based computers should remove HIMEM.SYS from their CONFIG.SYS files before proceeding.

386MAX

After running the 386MAX Install program, you'll be asked if you want to maximize your computer. The Maximize program, which can also be run at the DOS prompt, evaluates your device drivers and memory-resident programs and then loads them into UMBs in their optimum configuration. If you add another device driver or memory-resident program to your computer, simply run the Maximize program again. It's that easy.

386MAX changes CONFIG.SYS in the following ways. Note that new lines and changes are displayed in *italics*.

```
device=c:\386max\386max.sys pro=c:\386max\386max.pro
device=c:\dos\himem.sys
dos=high
files=30
buffers=20
shell=c:\dos\command.com c:\dos\ /p
stacks=0,0
device=c:\386max\386load.sys size=31712 prgreg=2 flexframe
    prog=c:\mouse\mouse.sys /c1
```

Above, 386MAX has installed a command that loads itself first as the memory manager for your computer. When 386MAX loads, it reads a profile report it generated when optimizing your computer. The profile contains settings that tell 386MAX how to load device drivers and memory-resident software for the best overall performance. Note that loading this device driver first will cause the HIMEM.SYS driver to report an error when it loads. Feel free to delete the command that loads the HIMEM.SYS device driver, because 386MAX is an extended and expanded memory manager and gives you access to the HMA just as HIMEM.SYS did. Better still, place a Rem command in front of the command that loads the HIMEM.SYS device driver.

The last command loads the mouse device driver into a UMB. (This command is split into two lines in the listing.) 386MAX uses its own device driver, 386LOAD.SYS, to load other device drivers into UMBs. The Maximize program has already added all the proper options to enable 386LOAD.SYS to load the mouse device driver into a UMB. This certainly saves time over manually adding options to DOS 5's Devicehigh command.

386MAX changes AUTOEXEC.BAT in the following ways. New lines and changes are in *italics*.

```
@echo off
prompt $p$g
path c:\dos;c:\batch;c:\util
set temp=c:\temp
c:\386max\386load size=6208 prgreg=4 flexframe prog=doskey
```

386MAX uses the 386LOAD.COM program to load memory-resident programs into UMBs. The Maximize program has added all the proper switches to load Doskey into a UMB.

386LOAD.SYS and 386LOAD.COM might seem bulky compared to DOS's Devicehigh and Loadhigh commands. They are. But the Maximize program adds all the proper options to load device drivers and memory-resident programs into UMBs for you; if you add any device drivers or memory-resident programs in the future, simply run Maximize again. (The options added above are all explained in the 386MAX manual.)

Will DOS's Devicehigh and Loadhigh work with 386MAX? Yes, if you add the umb option to the Dos command (*dos=high,umb*). After that, you can use Devicehigh and Loadhigh with 386MAX as you wish.

This is close to perfect, but more improvements are possible. Skip ahead to the section titled "Basic Memory Strategy."

MOVE'EM

MOVE'EM's installation is simple, and the Install program will put the command that loads MOVE'EM in the proper position in your CONFIG.SYS file. But MOVE'EM lacks a spiffy Maximize program like 386MAX. You must manually load all your device drivers and memory-resident programs into UMBs. To do so, follow the steps listed in the MOVE'EM manual and summarized here:

1. Use the MOVE'EM.SYS and MOVE'EM.COM programs to load your device drivers and memory-resident programs into UMBs. Specify the getsize option in the following format for CONFIG.SYS:

   ```
   device=c:\move'em\move'em.sys getsize prog=c:\mouse\mouse.sys
   ```

   You must also use the getsize option in AUTOEXEC.BAT:

   ```
   c:\move'em\move'em.com getsize prog=doskey
   ```

2. Reboot your computer.

3. Type the command *c:\move'em\move'em summary* to see a "Suggested Action" for each device driver and memory-resident program. This involves replacing the getsize option with the size of the device driver or memory-resident program.

4. Follow the suggestions, and edit CONFIG.SYS and AUTO-EXEC.BAT accordingly.

5. Reboot your computer again.

These steps aren't as complex as they sound, but they certainly aren't as nice as the Maximize program. (Actually, it's kind of nostalgic: QEMM-386 and 386MAX users used to follow the same procedure until enough users complained about it.)

The following CONFIG.SYS file displays the final result of MOVE'EM's efforts. New lines and changes are noted in *italics*.

```
device=c:\dos\himem.sys
device=c:\emm.sys at 258
device=c:\move'em\move'em.mgr
dos=high
files=30
buffers=20
shell=c:\dos\command.com c:\dos\   /p
stacks=0,0
device=c:\move'em\move'em.sys prog=c:\mouse\mouse.sys /c1
```

Note that MOVE'EM's memory manager is MOVE'EM.*MGR*; MOVE'EM.SYS loads device drivers into UMBs. Also, if you use MOVE'EM on an 8088/8086-based computer, you should remove the Dos command and the command that loads the HIMEM.SYS device driver. An 8088/8086-based computer has no extended memory and therefore cannot support an HMA.

Here is MOVE'EM's AUTOEXEC.BAT. New lines and changes are noted in *italics*.

```
@echo off
prompt $p$g
path c:\dos;c:\batch;c:\util
set temp=c:\temp
c:\move'em\move'em.com size=6208 prog=doskey
```

MOVE'EM.COM is used to load memory-resident programs, such as Doskey, into UMBs. The size value was determined using the techniques described above and in the MOVE'EM manual. (It really only took about three minutes and two computer reboots.)

The question arises: Can you use DOS 5's Devicehigh and Loadhigh commands with MOVE'EM? The answer is no. But still, being able to load device drivers and memory-resident programs into UMBs at all is more than DOS 5 allows on an 80286-based computer. Please skip ahead to the section titled "Basic Memory Strategy."

QEMM-386

QEMM-386's Install program copies all QEMM-386's programs (and the Manifest program) to your hard disk. Because you answered *yes* to all the questions, the QEMM-386 installation program adds the command that loads the QEMM386.SYS device driver in your CONFIG.SYS file and adds the QEMM subdirectory to the search path in your AUTOEXEC.BAT file. That's okay for now. Edit CONFIG.SYS, and place *rem* in front of the command that loads HIMEM.SYS. (This will prevent an error message when your computer boots.)

At the DOS prompt, run QEMM-386's Optimize program to properly configure your computer to load device drivers and memory-resident programs into UMBs. Type *optimize* at the DOS prompt, and follow the instructions on the screen. Your computer will reboot several times. Return here when you've finished.

The Optimize program evaluates your computer and the device drivers and memory-resident software loaded by CONFIG.SYS and AUTOEXEC.BAT. Optimize then configures QEMM-386 to load your device drivers and memory-resident programs into UMBs, taking care of all the options for you.

Optimize changes the two sample files as follows. New lines and changes are in *italics*.

QEMM-386's CONFIG.SYS file looks like this:

```
device=c:\qemm\qemm386.sys ram
rem device=c:\dos\himem.sys
dos=high
files=30
buffers=20
shell=c:\dos\command.com c:\dos\  /p
stacks=0,0
device=c:\qemm\loadhi.sys /r:1 c:\mouse\mouse.sys /c1
```

The QEMM-386.SYS device driver loads first, managing your expanded and extended memory and giving DOS access to the HMA.

The mouse device driver is loaded into a UMB by means of the QEMM-386 LOADHI.SYS device driver, which works like DOS 5's Devicehigh command. (But because LOADHI.SYS isn't an internal DOS 5 command, you must specify its path.)

Optimize changes AUTOEXEC.BAT as follows. New lines and changes are noted in *italics*.

```
@echo off
prompt $p$g
path c:\qemm;c:\dos;c:\batch;c:\util
set temp=c:\temp
c:\qemm\loadhi /r:3 doskey
```

QEMM-386 uses the LOADHI.COM program to load memory-resident programs into UMBs. Again, because LOADHI.COM is not an internal DOS 5 command, you must specify a full path.

The Optimize program adds LOADHI.SYS and LOADHI.COM commands, as well as any necessary options. If you add device drivers or memory-resident programs in the future, simply run the Optimize program again. (If you prefer, you can perform these operations manually with the instructions provided in the QEMM-386 Manual.)

Note that Optimize adds the QEMM subdirectory to your computer's search path. You can remove that subdirectory from your computer's search path if you like. Consider, however, creating batch files to run QEMM-386's support programs (QEMM.COM and MFT.EXE).

What about Devicehigh and Loadhigh? Will they still work? Yes, but you need to specify the umb option after the Dos command, as in *dos=high,umb*. After that, you can use Devicehigh and Loadhigh with QEMM-386 just as you do with DOS 5. Note that using the umb option after the Dos command causes any device drivers and memory-resident programs loaded with QEMM-386 commands to be loaded into conventional memory; so use only the DOS 5 Devicehigh and Loadhigh commands with the umb option.

You can make additional manual modifications to free more conventional memory in your computer with QEMM-386. Please skip ahead to the section titled "Basic Memory Strategy."

QRAM

The QRAM installation program copies QRAM's files to your hard disk and incorporates QRAM commands into your CONFIG.SYS and AUTOEXEC.BAT files. Your immediate next step should be to run the Optimize program to continue the configuration of your computer. At the DOS prompt, type *optimize*, and follow the directions that appear. Your computer will reboot several times before you've finished.

The Optimize program evaluates the device drivers and memory-resident programs in your computer and then uses QRAM's Loadhi commands to load device drivers and memory-resident programs into UMBs. Although the result isn't as memory efficient as the solution provided by 386MAX or QEMM-386, it's effective on 80286-based and 8088/8086-based computers that use DOS 5.

Note: If QRAM reports back "nothing to do," either you don't have LIM EMS 4.0 memory in your computer or the EMS card is not configured properly. Consult your EMS hardware manual for instructions on how to install and configure your EMS card.

The two sample files have been modified by Optimize as follows. New lines and changes are displayed in *italics*. (Note that the EMM.SYS device driver in line two is the expanded memory manager that comes with your EMS card.)

QRAM's CONFIG.SYS looks like this:

```
device=c:\dos\himem.sys
device=c:\intel\emm.sys at 258
device=c:\qram\qram.sys r:1
dos=high
files=30
buffers=20
shell=c:\dos\command.com c:\dos\ /p
stacks=0,0
device=c:\qram\loadhi.sys /r:1 c:\mouse\mouse.sys /c1
```

First comes the command to load the HIMEM.SYS device driver. (HIMEM.SYS should be used instead of the QEXT.SYS extended memory manager that comes with QRAM—HIMEM.SYS is more compatible with DOS 5.) Next comes the EMM device driver that manages expanded memory. (QRAM uses expanded memory to create UMBs.) QRAM.SYS is installed after the EMM device driver. Finally, the LOADHI.SYS device driver loads the mouse device driver into a UMB.

Note: You cannot use HIMEM.SYS on an 8088/8086-based computer, nor can you load part of DOS into the HMA with dos=high. Because the 8088/8086 can address only 1 MB of memory, 8088/8086-based computers can't access extended memory and therefore can't access the HMA.

QRAM's AUTOEXEC.BAT looks like this:

```
@echo off
prompt $p$g
path c:\qram;c:\dos;c:\batch;c:\util
set temp=c:\temp
c:\qram\loadhi /r:1 doskey
```

QRAM loads memory-resident programs into UMBs with the LOADHI.COM program. In this example, Loadhi is used to load Doskey into a UMB. Also, note that Optimize added the QRAM sub-directory to your computer's search path. You can remove that sub-directory from your computer's search path and instead run QRAM's support programs directly or, preferably, by means of batch files stored in a batch file subdirectory.

You can manually insert LOADHI.SYS and LOADHI.COM commands when you add new device drivers or memory-resident programs to your computer. You can also run the Optimize program again and let it reconfigure your computer for you.

Will DOS 5's Devicehigh and Loadhigh commands work under QRAM? They will! (But not on 8088/8086-based computers.) If you specify the Dos command's umb option, you can use the Devicehigh and Loadhigh commands to load device drivers and memory-resident programs into UMBs—just as on '386-based computers. (Refer to Chapter 6 for instructions—now that you know the secret.) QRAM can provide 80286-based computers with many of the memory-management capabilities that DOS 5 provides for '386-based computers.

BASIC MEMORY STRATEGY

When using a third-party memory manager with DOS 5, you must reach a compromise: Let DOS 5 do so much, and let the third-party memory manager do the rest. Deciding where to let the third-party memory manager take over can be aggravating, especially when you consider all the possibilities.

In the sections that follow, find the system most similar to yours, and use the information to develop an appropriate memory strategy.

'386-Based Computers Without Windows

The standard DOS 5 CONFIG.SYS file starts with three commands:

```
device=c:\dos\himem.sys
dos=high,umb
device=c:\dos\emm386.exe 512 ram
```

- Both 386MAX and QEMM-386 come with XMS and EMS memory managers, eliminating the first and third lines.

- Because both 386MAX and QEMM-386 also create UMBs, the Dos command no longer requires the umb option (unless you decide to use DOS 5 commands instead of the commands provided with 386MAX or QEMM-386).

With such changes, CONFIG.SYS now looks like this:

```
device=c:\386max\386max.sys options
rem device=c:\dos\himem.sys
dos=high
```

Or this:

```
device=c:\qemm\qemm.sys options
rem device=c:\dos\himem.sys
dos=high
```

The HIMEM.SYS device driver is no longer needed in these configurations. Here it's been commented out with the Rem command. And because the EMM386.EXE expanded memory emulator becomes redundant when you have 386MAX or QEMM-386, you can simply delete the command that loads EMM386.EXE.

Using this strategy, you should continue to load your device drivers and memory-resident programs into UMBs. For additional memory advantages, refer to the section titled "Loading Resources into UMBs."

'386-Based Computers with Windows

Windows will run in 386 enhanced mode with either QEMM-386 or 386MAX installed as described in this chapter. As long as you specify the various Windows options during installation and read any supplemental information regarding Windows, you should experience no problems—despite the fact that QEMM-386 and 386MAX simulate expanded memory with extended memory.

If you do encounter a problem starting Windows, use the /3 switch as follows:

```
win /3
```

That should get Windows up and running in 386 enhanced mode when QEMM-386 or 386MAX is installed. (To verify the Windows mode, pull down the Help menu in the Program Manager, and select the last item, About Program Manager.)

80286-Based Computers

On most 80286-based computers the memory strategy is twofold: The computer comes with extended memory. But to use UMBs and to use DOS applications that don't recognize extended memory, you need expanded memory.

On 80286-based computers, this means adding an EMS 4.0 memory card to your computer. Then install an expanded memory manager device driver. Finally install a memory manager device driver that creates the UMBs—either MOVE'EM.MGR or QRAM.SYS.

If you follow these steps, your CONFIG.SYS file should look similar to this:

```
device=c:\dos\himem.sys
device=c:\emm.sys options
device=c:\move'em\move'em.mgr options
dos=high
```

Or this:

```
device=c:\dos\himem.sys
device=c:\emm.sys options
device=c:\qram\qram.sys options
dos=high
```

Note that the subdirectories above are all assumed; you should specify the proper paths for all device drivers.

Finally you use your memory manager's programs to load device drivers and memory-resident programs into UMBs. If you're using QRAM with the Dos command's umb option, you can use the Devicehigh and Loadhigh commands to load device drivers and memory-resident programs into UMBs.

If you plan to run Windows, you should configure most of the memory on the memory expansion card as extended memory. (But be sure to leave enough expanded memory for applications that need expanded memory.)

8088/8086-Based Computers

The solutions for 8088/8086-based computers are, unfortunately, no better under DOS 5 than they were under DOS 4 or 3.3. The only option is to add a LIM EMS 4.0 memory expansion card to your computer and then backfill as much conventional memory as possible with expanded memory.

Both MOVE'EM and QRAM will load device drivers and memory-resident programs into UMBs if your 8088/8086-based computer has expanded memory. It's a simple solution, but it's better than no solution at all.

LOADING RESOURCES INTO UMBS

Third-party memory managers have two advantages over DOS 5: They can load system resources into UMBs, and they can "steal" video memory. The result: more conventional memory for your computer.

What are system resources anyway? Well, they're those files, buffers, and storage places that DOS needs in order to operate. Unfortunately, they also occupy conventional memory. Here's a list of common system resources and the amount of memory each uses.

Resource	Conventional Memory Used
FCBs	None (needed only for compatibility; use the Files command under DOS 5 instead)
Files	About 53 bytes for each file
Lastdrive	About 80 bytes for each drive letter after E

It might seem silly to load these resources into UMBs when the space to be gained appears minimal. But when your computer is low on memory, every byte counts. The following sections describe each of these system resources in greater detail.

FCBs

File Control Blocks, or FCBs, were used by programs that operated under DOS version 1. Although DOS version 2.0 introduced a more efficient method of file handling, the Fcbs command was retained for compatibility. If you have a program that absolutely requires FCBs, use the Fcbs command. Otherwise, use the Files command.

QEMM-386 and QRAM have an FCBS.COM program, which can be used to load FCBs into an upper memory block. If, and only if, you have a program that refuses to run without the Fcbs command, use QEMM-386 or QRAM's FCBS.COM program with the Loadhi command to load the FCBs into an upper memory block. The technique is similar to the Files command, and it's fully illustrated in the QEMM-386 and QRAM manuals.

Files

The DOS Files command sets the number of files that DOS can have open at one time. DOS keeps track of open files by using a small amount of memory (about 53 bytes) called a *file handle*. DOS needs one file handle for each open file. Some database and accounting packages require that you set the number of files that DOS can have open to 32 or more. That's not a large amount of memory (about 1.6 KB), but every byte adds up.

The memory for file handles is allocated when your computer boots. DOS typically uses conventional memory for the file handles. QEMM-386 and QRAM come with a program called FILES.COM that can use memory from a UMB for the file handles. To use FILES.COM, follow these steps:

1. Place the following command in your CONFIG.SYS file:

   ```
   files=10
   ```

2. Place the following command in your AUTOEXEC.BAT file:

   ```
   c:\qemm\loadhi c:\qemm\files=40
   ```

These commands let DOS have up to 40 files open simultaneously. The memory for 30 file handles comes from a UMB, and the other 10 from conventional memory. Be sure to specify the correct path for QEMM-386's (or QRAM's) Loadhi and Files programs. In this example, the C:\QEMM subdirectory is assumed.

Lastdrive

The Lastdrive command allows you to set the highest available drive letter in your computer. DOS allows drive letters up to the letter E. Beyond that, you use the Lastdrive command to reserve more drive letters, all the way up through the letter Z. But you pay a price of about 80 bytes per drive letter beyond E.

Note: The Lastdrive command is also used for network drives and for those who use the Subst command to assign drive letters to subdirectories (which can be handy).

QEMM-386 and QRAM come with a program called LASTDRIV.COM, which allocates memory for additional drive letters from a UMB. You can use this program even if you have only drives up through the letter C.

To use LASTDRIV.COM, follow these steps:

1. Edit or insert the Lastdrive command in your CONFIG.SYS file. Set Lastdrive to the highest drive letter in your computer (and don't forget any RAM disks). For example,

   ```
   lastdrive=d
   ```

2. Add the following command near the top of your AUTOEXEC.BAT file:

   ```
   c:\qemm\loadhi c:\qemm\lastdriv=z
   ```

This command reserves drive letters up through Z without losing any conventional memory but still giving you the option to add those drives in the future. Be sure to use the proper path for Loadhi and Lastdrive. In this example, the C:\QEMM subdirectory is assumed.

Note: QEMM and QRAM come with a program called BUFFERS.COM. Do not use it—it is compatible only with DOS 2.X and DOS 3.X.

USING VIDEO MEMORY

Take another look at the typical computer's memory map. Refer to Figure 9-1. Above the 640 KB is what? More memory? True. But it's video memory, used by the EGA and VGA adapters for their high-resolution graphics. You can't run programs there. Or can you?

MDA, or monochrome video systems, use only 4 KB of RAM (in 80-column mode), starting at address 720,896. CGA systems use only 32 KB of RAM, starting at address 753,664. But both EGA and VGA use 96 KB of RAM, starting at address 655,360.

386MAX, QEMM-386, and QRAM include programs that can "steal" some VGA or EGA display memory and use the stolen video memory as conventional memory on computers that already have 640 KB of conventional memory. As long as you're willing to run your computer as if it had a CGA card instead of a VGA or an EGA card, you can increase DOS's conventional memory by 96 KB.

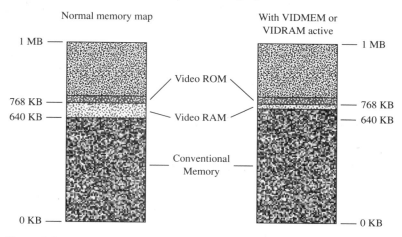

Figure 9-1. *How VIDMEM and VIDRAM can "steal" some video memory.*

The only drawback to this scenario is that graphics become taboo on your computer. Windows? Forget it! Don't even try to run programs that use graphics—your computer might lock up. But if you don't mind sacrificing your expensive graphics, here are the individual commands that steal EGA or VGA video memory for conventional memory.

386MAX

For 386MAX, the video memory is "stolen" by specifying the cga option with the command that loads 386MAX. This forces your computer into believing it has a CGA card instead of an EGA or a VGA. Voilá—you get that extra 96 KB of conventional memory and can move on to the bonus round. For example,

```
device=c:\386max\386max.sys pro=c:\386max\386max.pro cga
```

Here the assumption is that you have a VGA or an EGA card and want an extra 96 KB of conventional memory. The cga option gives you that extra memory. Also, if you want to simulate an MDA (monochrome) card, you can use the mono option, but that gives you only an extra 64 KB of conventional memory.

You could make such a change more effectively by editing 386MAX's profile file: 386MAX keeps its options in the file 386MAX.PRO. Use the DOS 5 Edit program to edit that file and add the word *cga* (or *mono*) as the last line in the file. Save the file, and then reboot your computer to steal all that video memory. (Refer to the 386MAX manual for more information on using the profile file to set options.)

Note: Run the Maximize program again when you've finished making this modification.

QEMM-386 and QRAM

QEMM-386 and QRAM owners can use the memory-resident VIDRAM program to convert VGA and EGA video memory to conventional memory. You can use the *vidram on* command to turn on video memory. When you're ready, turn it off with *vidram off*, which allows you to run your graphics programs again (but shrinks DOS back to below 640 KB).

If you use QEMM, you should first add the *vidramega* option to the Device command that loads QEMM in CONFIG.SYS. Then add the following two lines to your AUTOEXEC.BAT file:

```
c:\qemm\loadhi c:\qemm\vidram.com resident
c:\qemm\vidram on
```

The first command loads Vidram into a UMB and makes it resident. The second command turns on video memory, giving you up to 96 KB additional conventional memory. Wow.

The Vidram command works in nearly the same way for QRAM users, but QRAM lacks the vidramega option. Plus, QRAM users should specify *on* instead of *resident* when loading Vidram into a UMB. To do this, add these two lines to your AUTOEXEC.BAT file:

```
c:\qemm\loadhi c:\qemm\vidram.com on
c:\qemm\vidram on
```

The neat thing about the Vidram command is that you can use it to turn video memory off and get back your graphics. So if you suddenly decide that you want to use your VGA in the 50-row mode or run a graphics application, you can type *vidram off.*

Note: If you forget and try to run a graphics application, Vidram will remind you and present the option of turning itself off.

THE FINAL RESULTS

Using optimal configuration commands, the following are the final versions of the sample CONFIG.SYS and AUTOEXEC.BAT files presented early in this chapter. (Note that these are optimal configurations for my computer; yours might differ.) Further examples of other configurations are covered in Chapter 10.

Following each of the configurations is the amount of available memory remaining when my computer runs the configuration (as shown by the Mem command). Remember, your own CONFIG.SYS and AUTOEXEC.BAT files will be different, depending on your requirements. The files shown here are samples only (although they all work and produce the available memory indicated).

386MAX

CONFIG.SYS:

```
device=c:\386max\386max.sys pro=c:\386max\386max.pro
rem device=c:\dos\himem.sys
dos=high
files=30
buffers=20
shell=c:\dos\command.com c:\dos\ /p
stacks=0,0
device=c:\386max\386load.sys size=31712 prgreg=2 flexframe
    prog=c:\mouse\mouse.sys /c1
```

AUTOEXEC.BAT:

```
@echo off
prompt $p$g
path c:\dos;c:\batch;c:\util
set temp=c:\temp
c:\386max\386load size=6208 prgreg=2 flexframe prog=doskey
```

MEM:

```
753664 bytes total conventional memory
753664 bytes available to MS-DOS
737440 largest executable program size
```

MOVE'EM

CONFIG.SYS:

```
device=c:\dos\himem.sys
device=c:\emm.sys at 258
device=c:\move'em\move'em.mgr
dos=high
files=30
buffers=20
shell=c:\dos\command.com c:\dos\  /p
stacks=0,0
device=c:\move'em\move'em.sys prog=c:\mouse\mouse.sys /c1
```

AUTOEXEC.BAT:

```
@echo off
prompt $p$g
path c:\dos;c:\batch;c:\util
set temp=c:\temp
c:\move'em\move'em.com size=6208 prog=doskey
```

MEM:

```
655360 bytes total conventional memory
655360 bytes available to MS-DOS
625968 largest executable program size
```

QEMM

CONFIG.SYS:

```
device=c:\qemm\qemm386.sys ram vidramega
rem device=c:\dos\himem.sys
dos=high
files=10
buffers=20
lastdrive=c
shell=c:\dos\command.com c:\dos\  /p
stacks=0,0
device=c:\qemm\loadhi.sys /r:1 c:\mouse\mouse.sys /c1
```

AUTOEXEC.BAT:

```
@echo off
c:\qemm\loadhi c:\qemm\files=40
c:\qemm\loadhi c:\qemm\lastdriv=Z
c:\qemm\loadhi c:\qemm\vidram resident
c:\qemm\vidram on
prompt $p$g
path c:\dos;c:\batch;c:\util
set temp=c:\temp
c:\qemm\loadhi /r:3 doskey
```

MEM:

```
753664 bytes total conventional memory
753664 bytes available to MS-DOS
736800 largest executable program size
```

QRAM

CONFIG.SYS:

```
device=c:\dos\himem.sys
device=c:\emm.sys at 258
device=c:\qram\qram.sys r:1
dos=high
files=10
buffers=20
lastdrive=c
shell=c:\dos\command.com c:\dos\  /p
stacks=0,0
device=c:\qram\loadhi.sys /r:1 c:\mouse\mouse.sys /c1
```

AUTOEXEC.BAT:

```
@echo off
c:\qram\loadhi c:\qram\files=40
c:\qram\loadhi c:\qram\lastdriv=Z
c:\qram\loadhi c:\qram\vidram on
c:\qram\vidram on
prompt $p$g
path c:\dos;c:\batch;c:\util
set temp=c:\temp
c:\qram\loadhi /r:1 doskey
```

MEM:

```
753664 bytes total conventional memory
753664 bytes available to MS-DOS
725984 largest executable program size
```

Conclusion

You might be able to achieve better results than this. To find out, grab your memory manager and *read its manual.* You know the terms. You know what's where in memory. Now it will be easier to understand what the memory managers do and how you can take advantage of them.

SUMMARY

Memory management beyond what DOS 5 offers is possible and beneficial. Even on '386-based computers, third-party memory-management products will make kilobytes of conventional memory available for your applications, DOS, and Windows.

- 386MAX and QEMM-386 are two memory-management products for '386-based computers. They supplement the memory power DOS 5 gives you, managing extended and expanded memory and performing other memory services.

- MOVE'EM and QRAM are memory-management products for 80286-based and 8088/8086-based computers. They give 80286-based computers the ability to load device drivers and memory-resident programs into UMBs.

- Installation and optimization of the 386MAX, QEMM-386, and QRAM memory managers is greatly facilitated by the Maximize and Optimize programs. The Maximize and Optimize programs will fine-tune your computer's configuration for optimal memory performance.

- All four memory managers are compatible with Windows.

- QEMM-386 and QRAM have the ability to load your computer resources into UMBs, freeing even more conventional memory.

- On computers with 640 KB of conventional memory and EGA or VGA video adaptors, you can get up to 96 KB more conventional memory by using the VIDRAM.COM program that comes with QEMM-386 and QRAM, or the VIDMEM option with 386MAX. In some configurations, that's up to 736 KB of free conventional memory.

■ In the end, what you get out of your computer depends on what you have in it. All these memory managers will help in varying degrees, each of them offering that much more than what DOS 5 gives you. For a modest investment, you can get more free memory out of the same computer—without plugging in RAM chips.

Chapter 10

Setup Scenarios

The 386MAX manual mentions that, given only conventional and upper memory plus five device drivers and memory-resident programs, you can have up to 3840 possible loading configurations. Multiply that by some 50 million computers, and you can see why a book that promised the definitive CONFIG.SYS and AUTO-EXEC.BAT files for everyone would make the Los Angeles county phone book look like a pamphlet. Accordingly, this chapter focuses on several typical setup scenarios for a variety of situations and provides general and specific memory solutions for each. By using the setup that most closely resembles your own situation, and by taking advantage of the information in the other chapters in this book, your experiences with running out of memory will be, well...just a memory.

GENERAL SUGGESTIONS

No matter what your situation, you can take three steps that are guaranteed to help your computer get the most from memory:

- Add more memory whenever possible.

- Explore the DOS solutions, and consider a third-party memory manager.

- Install a RAM disk or a disk cache.

The following sections describe these steps in more detail.

8088/8086-Based Computers

DOS 5 memory solutions for 8088/8086-based computers are rare. Third-party memory managers are your best bet for solving your memory problems. Follow these steps.

1. **Add a LIM EMS 4.0 memory card to your computer.** Disable all but 256 KB of your conventional memory, and backfill the remaining 384 KB with expanded memory for a total of 640 KB of conventional memory.

2. **Pack the EMS card with as much memory as possible.** Buy at least 1 MB of memory. (If you find inexpensive memory, buy 2 MB.) A good strategy is to fill your EMS card to its maximum RAM potential. This prevents your having to open the computer's case again to add memory.

3. **Install your EMM device driver.** The EMM (expanded memory manager) device driver comes with your LIM EMS 4.0 memory card. Add the command that loads the EMM device driver in your CONFIG.SYS file.

4. **Install a third-party memory manager.** Although Chapter 9 contains memory solutions for 8088/8086-based computers, remember: The 8088/8086 has seen its peak, and memory solutions for it will soon disappear. When you upgrade, buy a '386-based computer.

5. **Take advantage of memory.** Some applications can directly use your expanded memory. If yours does not, consider creating a RAM disk or a disk cache. Refer to Chapter 7 for more information.

80286-Based Computers

Although no amount of software will give an 80286 the memory-management capabilities of a '386, you can enhance memory management through the following steps:

1. **Add extended memory to your computer.** Most 80286-based computers come with 1 MB of RAM: 640 KB of conventional memory and 384 KB of extended memory. Some programs (such as Windows) and utilities (such as RAM disks and disk caches) will use extended memory. For RAM disks and disk caches, extended memory is great! If you want a larger RAM

disk, buy extended memory for your 80286-based computer.
But this is only half the solution.

2. **Add a LIM EMS 4.0 memory card to your computer.** And
backfill as much conventional memory as possible.

3. **Pack the EMS card with as much memory as possible.** Most
EMS cards come with 512 KB of RAM. However, I suggest you
pack the card full of RAM immediately. This prevents your
having to open the computer's case again to add memory.

4. **Install your memory-manager device drivers.** Under DOS 5,
you'll need three memory-manager device drivers: HI-
MEM.SYS, the EMM device driver that came with your EMS
card, and the third-party memory-management device driver.
The coordination of these three memory managers is covered
in Chapter 9.

5. **Use the memory capabilities of DOS 5.** For an 80286-based
computer, load part of DOS into the HMA using the Dos command. If you've installed QRAM, you can also use the Dos
command's umb option. Next use the Devicehigh and Loadhigh commands to load device drivers and memory-resident
programs into UMBs.

6. **Load device drivers and memory-resident programs into
UMBs.** With the third-party memory manager, you can load
your device drivers and memory-resident programs into
UMBs. If the memory manager allows it, you can also load system resources into UMBs or "steal" video memory to add to
conventional memory.

7. **Take advantage of the new memory.** Some applications will
take immediate advantage of your expanded memory, whereas
others might need your extended memory. If no applications
use expanded or extended memory, create a RAM disk and a
disk cache to improve your computer's performance.

'386-Based Computers

DOS 5 and third-party memory managers offer the most benefits to '386-based computers. Follow these steps:

1. **Add extended memory to your computer.** Be sure all the memory you add is installed on the motherboard or in a special 32-bit memory card slot. Add as much memory as you can afford. (And remember to add it in the increments that are appropriate for your computer or memory board.)

2. **Use the DOS 5 memory-management commands.** First install the HIMEM.SYS extended memory device driver, then use the Dos command to load part of DOS into the HMA and prepare DOS for the UMBs, and finally install the EMM386.EXE device driver to create the UMBs or simulate expanded memory or both. Or you can use third-party memory managers to take the place of both HIMEM.SYS and EMM386.EXE. The Dos command is still required to load part of DOS into the HMA, but the umb option needs to be specified only if you're using the DOS Devicehigh and Loadhigh commands instead of the memory manager's counterparts.

3. **Load device drivers and memory-resident programs into UMBs.** If your third-party memory manager supports it, also load your system resources into UMBs. (Refer to Chapter 9.)

4. **Choose your computer's configuration.** Use EMM386.EXE to simulate expanded memory with extended memory if any of your applications require expanded memory. Sometimes a compromise must be reached: For example, maintain 2 MB of extended memory for a RAM disk, and use the rest to simulate expanded memory. Make your decision, and configure your computer accordingly.

   If you're not going to be using graphics, consider using extra EGA or VGA video memory to extend the DOS conventional memory limit. Both 386MAX and QEMM-386 let you do this. (Refer to the section "Using Video Memory" in Chapter 9.)

5. Take advantage of memory. Start working with applications that use extended or expanded memory. If you have memory left over, consider creating a RAM disk or a disk cache. (The benefits of each are covered in Chapter 7.)

SCENARIOS

On the following pages, you'll find descriptions of five sample computers: their hardware and software configurations, as well as complementary CONFIG.SYS and AUTOEXEC.BAT files that serve as possible solutions to memory problems. From these examples, apply the solutions to your own situation and computer.

386 Windows Computer

Description: A Compaq DESKPRO with an 80386 microprocessor and 2 MB of RAM. Windows requires at least 2 MB total memory in a '386-based computer to run in 386 enhanced mode. But the more memory you add, the faster Windows runs.

Strategy: Add 2 MB of memory to your computer, bringing the total amount of RAM to 4 MB.

Steps: Add two 1-MB memory modules to the DESKPRO's memory card. These memory modules are not DIPs, SIPs, or SIMMs, but actual cards that plug into the DESKPRO's memory card. It's safest to purchase these memory modules directly from Compaq rather than from a third-party vendor.

Note: After upgrading this computer, or any time you add extended memory to an 80286-based or '386-based computer, you'll see a memory error message when your computer boots. To fix the error, simply run your computer's Setup program to tell your computer about the new memory.

To use Windows on this computer, you'll want to configure all of memory as extended memory. But to have as much free conventional memory as possible, you'll want to load device drivers and memory-resident programs into UMBs.

This computer's CONFIG.SYS starts with the following three lines:

```
device=c:\windows\himem.sys
dos=high,umb
device=c:\dos\emm386.exe noems
```

HIMEM.SYS is an extended memory manager. The Dos command loads part of DOS into the HMA and prepares DOS for the UMBs. Then the EMM386.EXE expanded memory emulator creates those upper memory blocks but doesn't use any extended memory to simulate expanded memory.

At this point, you use the Devicehigh command to load your device drivers, such as MOUSE.SYS, SMARTDRV.SYS, and RAM-DRIVE.SYS, into UMBs.

When you install Windows, the Windows Setup program will probably create a large disk cache for you. Set the size of the disk cache at 512 KB or lower. Also, consider creating a small (64-KB or 128-KB) RAM disk, and use it to store DOS 5's and Windows' temporary files.

In the future, you could add more memory and take advantage of it with a somewhat larger disk cache and a larger RAM disk. For example, if you add another 2 MB of memory, you could create a 2-MB RAM disk to hold an important Windows application. With such an improvement you would notice a great increase in speed.

386 DOS Computer

Description: A Dell System 310 with an 80386 microprocessor and 4 MB of RAM.

Strategy: Run DOS 5, DESQview, and the QEMM-386 utilities to get the most out of conventional memory. The computer will then excel at running memory-hungry applications such as AutoCAD and will have plenty of room for a RAM disk.

Steps: To add more memory to this computer, you must purchase a special memory expansion card from Dell. The memory expansion card plugs into a special 32-bit memory slot and comes with an extra 2 MB of RAM, giving the computer a total of 6 MB of RAM.

DESQview uses only expanded memory. In addition to managing extended memory, allowing DOS to access the HMA, and creating UMBs, QEMM-386 will use all extended memory to simulate expanded memory. However, this computer requires a 2-MB RAM disk, which works best in extended memory. Therefore, QEMM-386 must be directed to leave 2 MB of extended memory. Here is the CONFIG.SYS file for this configuration:

```
device=c:\qemm\qemm386.sys ram vidramega extmem=2048
dos=high
buffers=20
files=10
lastdrive=d
device=c:\qemm\loadhi.sys c:\dos\ramdrive.sys 2048 /e
```

In this example, QEMM386.SYS is installed first using the Device command; HIMEM.SYS and EMM386.EXE are not needed. QEMM386.SYS is followed by several options: ram, which creates the UMBs; vidramega, which "steals" 96 KB of VGA video memory for conventional memory; and extmem=2048, which leaves 2 MB of extended memory for use as a RAM disk.

Part of DOS is loaded into the HMA with the Dos command above, and it seems as though the Files and Lastdrive commands are a little low—but they're actually loaded into UMBs by special QEMM-386 programs in the AUTOEXEC.BAT file. (Refer to Chapter 9.)

Finally QEMM-386's LOADHI.SYS program loads the RAM-DRIVE.SYS device driver into a UMB. Note that the 2-MB RAM disk is created in extended memory—the extended memory that was left by QEMM.SYS at the start of the CONFIG.SYS file.

386 General-Purpose Computer

Description: An Ergo Brick 80386SX portable with 2 MB of RAM and VGA graphics.

Strategy: Upgrade the computer to its full 8-MB potential.

Steps: Install six 1-MB 80-nanosecond or 100-nanosecond SIMMs on the motherboard.

This computer needs to be flexible: At times it's a DOS 5 computer that has expanded memory. But because this computer also runs graphics applications and—occasionally—Windows, it's best to select 386MAX, which sets up CONFIG.SYS as follows:

```
device=c:\386max\386max.sys pro=c:\386max\386max.pro
dos=high,umb
```

In this example, the Device command loads 386MAX.SYS into memory. The file 386MAX.PRO contains 386MAX options. (During 386MAX's installation, it was indicated that the computer might run Windows; therefore, all 386MAX options have been set properly for Windows.)

The Dos command loads part of DOS into the HMA, and the umb option prepares DOS for the UMBs. Since 386MAX is compatible with DOS 5's Devicehigh and Loadhigh commands, you can use Devicehigh and Loadhigh to load device drivers and memory-resident programs into UMBs.

Notice that the vidmem option for 386MAX is not specified on this computer. Although it would give an extra 96 KB to conventional memory, it would be incompatible with graphics programs and Windows.

286 Windows Computer

Description: An original IBM AT computer with an 80286 microprocessor and 512 KB of RAM.

Strategy: Purchase an Intel Above Board. The Above Board can supply the computer with both extended and expanded memory. To use Windows, your computer needs at least 256 KB of extended memory, but you'd like to backfill with expanded memory to take advantage of LIM EMS 4.0–compatible applications.

Steps: Pack the Above Board with as much memory as it can hold (2 MB). Configure 1 MB as extended memory and the other megabyte as expanded memory. The expanded memory will be used for backfill and to create the UMBs, and the extended memory will be used by Windows.

Three device drivers are needed to manage all this memory: An extended memory manager, an expanded memory manager, and a memory manager to create the UMBs from expanded memory. Presently, QRAM makes a good choice for this computer: Not only can QRAM load device drivers and memory-resident programs into UMBs, but QRAM is also compatible with DOS 5's Devicehigh and Loadhigh commands, which normally work only on '386-based computers. Here's the CONFIG.SYS file for this computer:

```
device=c:\windows\himem.sys
device=c:\intel\emm.sys at 258
device=c:\qram\qram.sys r:1
dos=high,umb
buffers=10
files=10
lastdrive=c
devicehigh=c:\windows\mouse.sys
```

HIMEM.SYS is the extended memory manager and allows DOS to access the HMA. Next EMM.SYS is Intel's expanded memory manager. QRAM's memory manager, QRAM.SYS, maps expanded memory into the vacant areas in upper memory to create UMBs.

The Dos command loads part of DOS into the HMA and prepares DOS for the UMBs. QRAM.SYS creates the UMBs. The Devicehigh and Loadhigh commands can now be used on this 80286-based computer to load device drivers and memory-resident programs into the UMBs.

The Files and Lastdrive commands are deliberately set to low values; counterpart QRAM commands are specified in AUTO-EXEC.BAT to create file handles and space for additional drive letters in UMBs.

Spreadsheet Computer

Description: Spreadsheets require a lot of memory. Lotus 1-2-3 version 2.2 can use up to 640 KB of conventional memory and 4 MB of expanded memory. To check your memory usage, type the /, *Worksheet, Global* command while running Lotus 1-2-3 version 2.2. The memory usage is displayed in the top center of the screen.

If you load Lotus 1-2-3 version 2.2 on the typical DOS 5 computer, with part of DOS loaded into the HMA and a few device drivers loaded into UMBs, you might see up to 415 KB of available conventional memory, plus as much expanded memory as you've installed in your computer or is being simulated by extended memory. (Remember, Lotus 1-2-3 was the original inspiration for expanded memory.)

Strategy: The best way to add expanded memory to a '386-based computer is to add extended memory and then simulate expanded memory with extended memory, using EMM386.EXE or a third-party memory manager.

Steps: For example, suppose you have the very fast Everex Step 486/25 to make Lotus 1-2-3 sizzle. The computer has 4 MB of RAM on a memory expansion card in a special 32-bit memory card slot. To simulate 4 MB of expanded memory, the following lines are used in CONFIG.SYS:

```
device=c:\dos\himem.sys
dos=high,umb
device=c:\dos\emm386.exe 4096 ram
```

HIMEM.SYS is installed first, and then the Dos command is used to load part of DOS into the HMA and prepare DOS for the UMBs. The EMM386.EXE device driver is used to simulate 4 MB of expanded memory using extended memory, as well as to create the UMBs (thanks to the ram option).

If this computer had a VGA or EGA graphics card, you could use one of the third-party memory managers to steal some of the video memory for conventional memory. (But note that you would have to reconfigure Lotus 1-2-3 to run in CGA mode.)

Networked System

Description: A 1-MB 80286-based computer hooked up to a network—a "diskless workstation." All hard-disk storage is provided by the network file server. This computer does have a 1.2-MB floppy disk drive, which is used to boot the computer. There's room for extended memory, as well as expansion slots into which you could plug a LIM EMS 4.0 memory card.

Strategy: Add expanded memory and move the network device drivers into UMBs. DOS cannot do this alone on an 80286-based computer, so you need a third-party memory manager plus the EMS memory card. You must create an interesting boot disk containing the network device drivers and network programs, DOS programs, and memory managers. But by eliminating unneeded files there should be enough space on a 1.2-MB disk to hold all the files necessary to boot the computer and connect it to the network.

Steps: Install an EMS card in your computer. The EMS card should have as much memory as possible, with a minimum of 512 KB.

On the software side, install the HIMEM.SYS extended memory manager to allow DOS to access the HMA. Next install your expanded memory manager and the third-party memory manager. Use the third-party memory manager's commands to load your network device drivers into UMBs. If you use QRAM, you can use DOS 5's Devicehigh and Loadhigh commands instead (which saves on boot disk space). For example,

```
device=a:\dos\himem.sys
device=a:\emm.sys at 258
device=a:\qram\qram.sys r:1
dos=high,umb
```

The AUTOEXEC.BAT file will contain the following commands:

```
loadhigh a:\novell\ipx.com
loadhigh a:\novell\net5.com
```

QRAM is used in this example because QRAM is compatible with the Dos command's umb option. Now use the DOS 5 Loadhigh command to load the network shell into a UMB.

In the future you could add extended memory and create a large RAM disk. For example, if you added 4 MB of extended memory, you could use the RAMDRIVE.SYS device driver to create a 4-MB RAM disk. Programs such as Windows and other disk-intensive applications could then be transferred from the server to the RAM disk and would run very fast. After adding the extended memory, you'd place the following command in your CONFIG.SYS file (after the memory management commands):

```
devicehigh=a:\dos\ramdrive.sys 4096 /e
```

Devicehigh loads the RAM-disk device driver into a UMB; 4096 is the size of the RAM disk (4 MB); and the /e switch creates the RAM disk in extended memory.

SUMMARY

Getting the best performance out of your computer requires adding memory to your computer, figuring out what type of memory your applications need, and then configuring the memory accordingly.

DOS 5 works best on '386-based computers. Conventional memory can be freed by loading part of DOS into the HMA and loading device drivers and memory-resident programs into UMBs. Extended memory is available for those applications that require it. The extended memory can be used to simulate expanded memory if any of your applications require expanded memory.

For 80286-based and 8088/8086-based computers, the DOS 5 solutions are more limited, but third-party memory managers can give you the same power—and sometimes more—than what DOS 5 provides.

The best solution for 8088/8086-based or 80286-based computers is a combination of DOS 5 and a third-party memory manager. Consider the following:

- How much memory can I afford to add to my computer?

- Can I add and use a LIM EMS 4.0 memory card in my 80286-based or 8088/8086-based computer? (And if you do, use it to backfill conventional memory.)

- What type of memory do my applications require? Do they need extended or expanded memory, and how much of each?

- Which CONFIG.SYS commands load my extended and expanded memory managers?

- Part of DOS should always be loaded into the HMA on 80286-based and '386-based computers. (This is an answer, not a question. Unfortunately, the HMA doesn't exist on 8088/8086-based computers.)

- Device drivers and memory-resident programs should be loaded into UMBs when possible.

- If your third-party memory manager supports it, load your system resources into UMBs.

- If you have an EGA or a VGA graphics card but don't need EGA or VGA graphics, let a third-party memory manager steal some of your graphics card's video memory for conventional memory.

- After you're satisfied with CONFIG.SYS and AUTOEXEC.BAT, *leave them alone!*

It takes time and trouble to get everything "just right" in your CONFIG.SYS and AUTOEXEC.BAT files. This is why those installation programs that change your CONFIG.SYS and AUTOEXEC.BAT files can be so annoying. As a final suggestion, copy your final, pristine CONFIG.SYS and AUTOEXEC.BAT files to your DOS subdirectory. Use the Attrib command to make them read-only, as follows:

```
C:\DOS>attrib c:\dos\autoexec.bat +r
C:\DOS>attrib c:\dos\config.sys +r
```

These files will serve as backups if anything happens to the original files.

Appendix A

Glossary

'386 An Intel 80386, 80386SX, i486, i486SX, or similar microprocessor. Thanks to the advanced, built-in memory-mapping capabilities of these chips, DOS can do wondrous things with memory —without extra hardware.

80286 An Intel 80286 or similar microprocessor. Although this chip can access up to 16 MB of memory, it lacks the memory-mapping capabilities of the '386 family.

8088/8086 An Intel 8088 or 8086, NEC V20 or V30, or similar microprocessor. DOS doesn't have a real memory solution for these chips, but third-party memory managers in combination with a LIM EMS 4.0 memory expansion card will work wonders for computers that use these chips.

address A location in memory. Each location in memory has an address—a specific place somewhere in conventional memory, upper memory, or extended memory.

address space The total amount of memory a microprocessor can access. The 8088/8086 has a 1-MB address space, the 80286 has a 16-MB address space, and the '386 has a 4096-MB address space (except for the 80386SX, which has an address space of 16 MB).

backfill The process of an EMS memory card mapping expanded memory into conventional memory to bring the total amount of conventional memory up to 640 KB. A strategy worth taking on 8088/8086-based and 80286-based computers to get the most from EMS 4.0 is to disable all but 256 KB of conventional memory. Let a LIM EMS 4.0 memory card map expanded memory into the disabled 384 KB. This 384-KB region acts like one big page frame; expanded memory can be mapped in and out of this region.

BIOS Basic Input/Output System. The BIOS is a set of routines stored in ROM chips. The routines work closely with the computer's hardware to support the transfer of information between parts of your computer, such as memory, disk drives, and the monitor. The BIOS is invisible to computer users—only programmers need to access the BIOS.

bit A binary digit, either a 1 or a 0 in the binary number system. A bit is the smallest unit of information a computer can handle.

byte A group of 8 bits used to represent a value from 0 through 255, which in turn ultimately represents a single alphanumeric character, graphics character, or special control character. Therefore, a byte can be thought of as a single character of information.

conventional memory The lower 640 KB of memory, from memory location 0 through 655,359. This is where DOS and applications normally run.

device driver A control program that permits a computer to communicate with a device such as a disk drive or a mouse.

Devicehigh The DOS 5 command that loads device drivers into upper memory blocks. It's roughly equivalent to the Device command, with the addition of the size option.

DIP Dual In-line Package. The traditional RAM chip package.

disk cache A portion of memory that stores information read from disk. If the computer needs that information again, it reads it from the disk cache rather than from disk.

DRAM Dynamic Random Access Memory. An inexpensive type of memory chip that needs periodic refreshing ("recharging"). The majority of memory chips in a computer are DRAMs.

EMM *See* expanded memory manager.

EMS *See* expanded memory specification.

expanded memory Memory that is not normally in a microprocessor's address space. Think of it as a pool of extra memory that DOS can access via an EMS device driver.

expanded memory manager A device driver that implements the software portion of the expanded memory specification (EMS). Although EMS systems typically require additional hardware, EMMs written for '386 microprocessors can use the advanced memory-mapping capabilities of these chips to simulate expanded memory by using extended memory.

expanded memory specification A technique for adding memory to IBM PCs and compatible computers; also known as LIM (Lotus-Intel-Microsoft) EMS.

extended memory Memory above 1 MB on 80286-based and '386-based computers. It is accessible only when the microprocessor is in protected mode. Because DOS runs in real mode, extended memory is not usually available to DOS applications. *See also* extended memory specification.

extended memory specification A specification that defines a software interface to allow real-mode applications to use extended memory. The management of extended memory is provided by a device driver called an extended memory manager. DOS 5 provides the HIMEM.SYS device driver for managing extended memory.

gigabyte (GB) Roughly 1 billion bytes.

high-DOS memory Another term for upper memory.

high memory area The first 64 KB of extended memory on an 80286-based or '386-based computer. The HIMEM.SYS device driver lets DOS access the high memory area (HMA). The Dos command loads part of DOS 5 into the HMA, freeing about 50 KB of conventional memory.

HMA *See* high memory area.

interleaving A method of speeding memory access by splitting memory into two regions. One region is refreshed while the other is accessed. This improves the computer's overall performance.

kilobyte (KB) Roughly 1000 bytes.

LH An abbreviation for the Loadhigh command. *See* Loadhigh.

LIM EMS 4.0 The Lotus-Intel-Microsoft expanded memory specification, version 4.0, the most current version of LIM EMS. It allows up to 32 MB of expanded memory and allows for large chunks of mappable conventional memory to be swapped in and out of expanded memory. This is how some operating environments (such as DESQview) allow multitasking.

load high To load a device driver or memory-resident program into an upper memory block (UMB). *See also* Devicehigh, Loadhigh, upper memory blocks.

Loadhigh The DOS command that loads a memory-resident program into an upper memory block. Loadhigh can be abbreviated as LH.

low-DOS memory Another term for conventional memory. *See* conventional memory.

megabyte (MB) Roughly 1 million bytes.

memory Circuitry that allows information to be stored and retrieved. There are two main types of memory: RAM and ROM. *See* RAM, ROM.

memory-resident program A program that remains in memory even when it's not running so that it can be quickly activated for a specific task while another application is running. Memory-resident programs are also known as terminate-and-stay-resident programs (TSRs). One big drawback of memory-resident programs is that they are usually loaded into conventional memory, but DOS 5 allows them to be loaded into upper memory blocks. *See* Loadhigh, upper memory blocks.

microprocessor A central processing unit (CPU) on a single chip. *See also* '386, 80286, 8088/8086.

motherboard The main circuit board inside a computer. The motherboard usually contains the microprocessor, RAM, ROM, and expansion slots.

motherboard memory Memory that can be installed directly on a computer's motherboard. This term once referred only to conventional memory. However, 80286-based and '386-based computers can have both conventional and extended memory installed on their motherboards. On '386-based computers, motherboard memory is faster and more useful than memory added by means of an expansion card (with the exception of cards designed for 32-bit expansion slots).

nanosecond One billionth of a second. The speed of RAM chips is measured in nanoseconds.

page A 16-KB bank of expanded memory.

page frame A 64-KB area in upper memory. Four 16-KB pages are mapped into the page frame by the expanded memory manager.

protected mode An operating mode of 80286 and '386 microprocessors that supports larger address spaces and more advanced features than real mode. Unfortunately, DOS operates in real mode, which means that 80286 and '386 chips must run in real mode to run DOS applications.

RAM Random Access Memory. Memory that can be read from or written to by the microprocessor.

RAM disk A simulated disk drive whose data is actually stored in RAM. A device driver, such as RAMDRIVE.SYS, can create a RAM disk in conventional, extended, or expanded memory. RAM disks are much faster than disk drives but have the disadvantage of losing their contents when the power goes off.

real mode An 80286 and '386 operating mode that is 8088/8086-compatible. In real mode, DOS treats 80286 and '386 microprocessors as if they're very fast 8088/8086 microprocessors.

reserved memory Another term for upper memory.

ROM Read Only Memory. A type of memory that contains instructions or information the microprocessor can read but cannot change.

shadow RAM The process of copying the contents of a computer's ROM or BIOS into faster RAM. This improves the computer's overall speed but can cause memory conflicts.

SIMM Single In-line Memory Module. A bank of RAM chips, all installed on a tiny expansion card about half the size of a small comb.

SIP Single In-line Package. A type of housing for a collection of memory chips in which all the legs of the chips protrude from one side of the package.

SRAM Static Random Access Memory. A type of memory that is faster than DRAM, primarily because it doesn't need to be refreshed. SRAMs are used in some computers to speed operations. Their expense prevents them from being commonly used as main memory.

TSR Terminate-and-stay-resident. Another name for a memory-resident program. *See* memory-resident program.

UMBs *See* upper memory blocks.

upper memory The area of memory between 640 KB and 1 MB. That 384 KB of memory is used to store video memory, installable ROMs, and the ROM BIOS. Programs cannot run in upper memory, but you can load device drivers and memory-resident programs into UMBs using the Devicehigh and Loadhigh commands. *See* Devicehigh, Loadhigh.

upper memory blocks Areas in upper memory not occupied by ROMs or video memory. The EMM386.EXE expanded memory emulator can map extended memory into these areas, creating upper memory blocks. DOS 5 needs a '386-based computer with at least 350 KB of extended memory for EMM386.EXE to do this. Device drivers and memory-resident programs can be loaded into UMBs with the Devicehigh and Loadhigh commands.

video memory Memory that stores the computer's display image.

wait state A pause that occurs when the microprocessor must wait for data from memory.

XMS *See* extended memory specification.

Appendix B

Command Summary

This appendix describes the commands that deal with memory and memory configuration.

CONFIGURATION COMMANDS
EMM386.EXE

EMM386.EXE creates UMBs on '386-based computers with at least 350 KB of extended memory. EMM386.EXE can also simulate expanded memory by making use of extended memory on '386-based computers.

```
device=[pathname]emm386.exe [mode] [memory] [options] [noems ¦ ram]
```

pathname indicates the path to the EMM386.EXE device driver, complete with optional drive letter and subdirectories.

mode is either *on*, *off*, or *auto*. This turns the EMM386.EXE device driver's expanded memory support on or off or sets it to automatic. Setting mode to *on* enables expanded memory support. Setting mode to *off* disables expanded memory support. The default is *auto*. Auto mode enables expanded memory support only when an application needs it.

memory is the amount (in kilobytes) of expanded memory to be simulated with extended memory. Values range from 16 (for 16 KB) through as much extended memory as is available. The maximum amount of simulated expanded memory is 32768 (for 32 MB), and the default is 256 (256 KB).

options represents the following options:

w=[on ¦ off]   Turns support for the Weitek coprocessor on or off.

175

m*x*	Gives the page frame address. The page frame address is controlled by *x* as shown:

1 = C000	8 = DC00
2 = C400	9 = E000
3 = C800	10 = 8000
4 = CC00	11 = 8400
5 = D000	12 = 8800
6 = D400	13 = 8C00
7 = D800	14 = 9000

frame=*address*	Where *address* is one of the four-digit hex values listed above.
a=*altregs*	Specifies the number of fast alternate register sets (used for multitasking) you want to allocate to EMM386.EXE. Values for *altregs* range from 0 through 254, with 7 as the default. Every alternate register set adds about 200 bytes to the size in memory of EMM386.EXE.
h=*handles*	Specifies the number of EMS handles to use for accessing expanded memory. Values for *handles* range from 2 to 255, with 64 as the default.
d=*nnn*	Indicates the amount of memory needed for DMA buffering. Values for *nnn* are in kilobytes and range from 16 through 256, with 16 as the default.

noems is used to create UMBs while not simulating any expanded memory with extended memory.

ram creates UMBs in addition to simulating expanded memory with extended memory.

Notes

■ The HIMEM.SYS device driver must be installed before you install EMM386.EXE.

■ *noems* and *ram* cannot both be specified.

Device=HIMEM.SYS

The HIMEM.SYS device driver manages all extended memory in the computer and allows DOS to access the HMA.

```
device=[pathname]himem.sys [options]
```

pathname indicates the path to the HIMEM.SYS device driver, complete with optional drive letter and subdirectories.

options represents the following optional switches:

/hmamin=*m*	Specifies the amount of memory (in kilobytes) a program must use before HIMEM.SYS allows the program to use the HMA. Values for *m* range from 0 through 63, with 0 as the default.
/numhandles=*n*	Specifies the number of extended memory block handles that can be used simultaneously. Values for *n* range from 1 through 128, with 32 as the default. Each additional handle requires about 6 bytes of conventional memory.
/int15=*xxx*	Allocates the specified amount of extended memory (in kilobytes) for the interrupt 15h interface. Values range from 64 through 65535, with 0 as the default.
/machine:*xxx*	Selects the proper A20 line handler (the program that allows DOS access to the HMA) to be used, depending on your computer. Values for each computer are listed in the DOS manual, although HIMEM.SYS usually selects the correct one.
/a20control:[*on* ¦ *off*]	Determines whether HIMEM.SYS will control the A20 line even if A20 was on when HIMEM.SYS was loaded. The default is *on*. If you specify *on*, HIMEM.SYS takes control of the A20 line only if A20 was off when HIMEM.SYS loaded.
/shadowram:[*on* ¦ *off*]	Specifies whether HIMEM.SYS should switch off shadow RAM. If your computer has less than 2 MB of memory, the default is *off*. Otherwise, the default is *on*.
/cpuclock:[*on* ¦ *off*]	Specifies whether HIMEM.SYS should affect the clock speed of your computer. If your computer's speed changes when you load HIMEM.SYS, specifying *on* might solve the problem. Enabling this switch slows down HIMEM.SYS (and therefore any program that uses extended memory). By default, this switch is *off*.

Notes

■ HIMEM.SYS should be the first device driver installed in your CONFIG.SYS file.

Device=RAMDRIVE.SYS

The RAMDRIVE.SYS device driver creates a RAM disk in either conventional, extended, or expanded memory.

```
device=[pathname]ramdrive.sys [size [sector [entries]]] [/e:/a]
```

pathname indicates the path to the RAMDRIVE.SYS device driver, complete with optional drive letter and subdirectories.

size is the size of the RAM disk in kilobytes. Values for *size* range from 16 through 4096 for a 16-KB through 4-MB RAM disk. When *size* isn't specified, a 64-KB RAM disk is created.

sector is the size of the RAM disk's sectors in bytes. Large sector sizes are good for large files, and small sector sizes are good for small files. Values for *sector* can be 128, 256, or 512, with 512 being the default. If you specify a sector size, you must also include a size for the RAM disk.

entries indicates the number of directory entries (places where DOS stores filenames) that RAMDRIVE.SYS will create in the RAM disk's root directory. Values for *entries* range from 2 through 1024, with 64 being the default. If you specify the number of entries, you must also specify a sector size and the size of the RAM disk.

/e or */a* directs RAMDRIVE.SYS to create the RAM disk in extended or expanded memory. If both switches are omitted, the RAM disk is created in conventional memory.

Notes

■ You must have enough memory to create the RAM disk. If you don't have enough memory to create a RAM disk of the specified size, RAMDRIVE.SYS creates a smaller RAM disk.

■ When the *sector* or *entries* parameter is specified, you must also specify all parameters that precede it.

■ Each RAM disk created is given the next-highest drive letter in your computer.

Device=SMARTDRV.SYS

The SMARTDRV.SYS device driver creates a disk cache on your computer by using either extended or expanded memory.

```
device=[pathname]smartdrv.sys [max [min]] [/a]
```

pathname indicates the path to the SMARTDRV.SYS device driver, complete with optional drive letter and subdirectories.

max specifies the maximum size for the disk cache in kilobytes. Values for *max* range from 128 through 8192 (for a 128-KB through an 8-MB disk cache), with 256 as the default.

min specifies the minimum size for the cache in kilobytes. Values for *min* should be less than those for *max*, all the way down to 0 (the default). Windows can dynamically reduce the size of the SMARTDRV.SYS disk cache to obtain more memory for Windows applications. When Windows quits, it returns the memory to SMARTDRV.SYS.

/a tells SMARTDRV.SYS to create the disk cache by using expanded memory. If */a* isn't specified, the cache is created in extended memory.

Notes

- It's best to create the cache in extended memory.

- To prevent Windows from reducing the size of the disk cache, specify the same value for both *min* and *max*.

Dos

The Dos command loads part of DOS into the HMA and prepares DOS for the UMBs created by EMM386.EXE.

```
dos=[high¦low][umb¦noumb]
```

The first option is either *high* or *low*. When *high* is specified, part of DOS is loaded into the HMA; *low* (the default) places DOS into conventional memory.

The second option is either *umb* or *noumb*. When *umb* is specified, DOS prepares for the UMBs and allows you to use the Devicehigh and Loadhigh programs; *noumb* (the default) doesn't prepare DOS for the UMBs. Devicehigh and Loadhigh cannot be used when *noumb* is specified.

Notes

■ This command works only when HIMEM.SYS has been installed.

■ The *umb* option works only on '386-based computers that have the EMM386.EXE device driver installed. Options must be separated with a comma.

Devicehigh

The Devicehigh command loads device drivers into UMBs.

```
devicehigh [size=hex][pathname] driver
```

size=hex is optional and indicates the size of the device driver (in hexadecimal). *hex* tells the Devicehigh command how much space the driver will occupy. (The size of the device driver is found by using the Mem /c command.)

pathname indicates the path to the device driver, complete with optional drive letter and subdirectories.

driver is the name of the device driver, followed by whatever switches the device driver requires. If the *size=hex* option is not used, an equal sign must be placed between the Devicehigh command and the name of the device driver.

Notes

■ You must create UMBs with EMM386.EXE and the Dos command before you can use Devicehigh.

■ If there isn't enough room for the device driver in upper memory, the device driver is loaded into conventional memory, as if the Device command had been used.

MS-DOS COMMANDS
EMM386.EXE

EMM386.EXE is both a device driver and a DOS command. As a command, it displays the current status of the EMS driver and turns expanded memory support on or off.

```
emm386 [on¦off¦auto][w=on¦w=off]
```

When used without any options, the Emm386 command displays the status of expanded memory support and the upper memory blocks in your system.

The first option is either *on, off,* or *auto.* The *on* option turns the EMM386.EXE device driver on, *off* turns it off, and *auto* activates auto mode. In auto mode, expanded memory support is enabled only when an application needs it. The default is *on.*

The second option is either *w=on* or *w=off* and is used to activate support for a Weitek math coprocessor. The default is *w=off.*

Notes

■ You cannot turn expanded memory support off when UMBs have been created.

Loadhigh

The Loadhigh command loads memory-resident programs into UMBs. It is an internal DOS command and can be abbreviated *lh.*

```
loadhigh [pathname]filename
```

pathname is the path to the memory-resident program, complete with optional drive letter and subdirectories.

filename is the name of a memory-resident program. It's followed by the switches or parameters that would typically follow it on the command line or in a batch file.

Notes

■ You must create UMBs with EMM386.EXE and the Dos command before you can use Loadhigh.

■ If there isn't enough room in upper memory, the memory-resident program is loaded into conventional memory.

Mem

The Mem command reports on the status of your computer's used
and free memory and, optionally, the contents of memory.

```
mem [/classify ¦ /program ¦ /debug] [¦ more]
```

When used without switches, the Mem command provides a summary of free and used conventional, expanded, and extended
memory in your system.

The Mem command's three optional switches are /classify, /pro-
gram, and /debug, which can be abbreviated /c, /p, and /d. Only one
switch can be specified at a time:

■ The /classify switch displays a brief summary of all programs
in conventional memory as well as in the upper memory area.

■ The /program switch provides a list of all programs in memory,
as well as their locations and sizes in hexadecimal.

■ The /debug switch displays the same information as the /pro-
gram switch but adds information and details about internal
DOS device drivers.

¦ more pipes the output of the Mem command through the DOS
More filter, which pauses the display after every screenful of text.

Index

Special Characters

183

Dan Gookin

Dan Gookin is a free-lance writer specializing in books and articles about MS-DOS and IBM Personal Computers. In addition to his writing duties and passion for Preston Sturges films, he hosts a Sunday radio talk show in the San Diego area about personal computers. Gookin is the coauthor (with Van Wolverton) of Supercharging MS-DOS, 3d Edition, published by Microsoft Press.

The manuscript for this book was prepared and submitted to Microsoft Press in electronic form. Text files were processed and formatted using Microsoft Word.

Principal word processor: Judith Bloch
Principal proofreader: Deborah Long
Principal typographer: Carolyn Magruder
Interior text designer: Kim Eggleston
Principal illustrator: Lisa Sandburg
Cover designer: Becky Johnson
Cover color separator: Precision Photo

Text composition by Microsoft Press in Times Roman with display type in Futura Heavy, using the Magna composition system and the Linotronic 300 laser imagesetter.

Printed on recycled paper stock.